641.564 BOV
Boven, Yvette van.
Home made summer
32148001798809

8/13

P9-DNC-840

YOU ARE MY SUNSHINE,
MY ONLY SUNSHINE
YOU MAKE ME HAPPY
WHEN SKIES ARE GRAY
YOU'LL NEVER KNOW DEAR
HOW MUCH I LOVE YOU
PLEASE DON'T TAKE
MY SUNSHINE AWAY

From "You Are My Sunshine," an American folk song
My sister and I loved to sing this song during family road trips.

641.564
BOV

3 2148 00179 8809

home made
summer

yvette van boven

photography:
oof verschuren

Middletown Public Library
700 West Main Rd.
Middletown, RI 02842

STEWART, TABORI & CHANG
NEW YORK

8/14/2013

handy:

* ALL RECIPES SERVE 4, UNLESS OTHERWISE INDICATED.

* 1 TBSP = 15 G   * 1 TSP = 5 G

* BAKING TIMES MAY BE LONGER OR SHORTER IN DIFFERENT OVENS. THE BAKING TIMES IN THIS BOOK ARE THEREFORE SUGGESTIONS. PLEASE RELY ON YOUR EXPERIENCE WITH YOUR OWN OVEN.

* I OFTEN USE CAGE-FREE EGGS (LARGE), BUT I MUCH PREFER USING FREE-RANGE OR ORGANIC EGGS.

* 1 LITER = 10 DL = 100 CL = 1000 ML

* ALWAYS USE FREE-RANGE OR, EVEN BETTER, ORGANIC MEAT. AND THIS IS MANDATORY!

YES! → THAT'S ME INDEED!
PHOTOGRAPHED BY OOF (110 YEARS AGO)

PUBLISHED IN 2012
BY STEWART, TABORI & CHANG. AN IMPRINT OF ABRAMS.

text, food styling, prop styling, design & illustrations:
YVETTE VAN BOVEN

photography: OOF VERSCHUREN
LIESKE VAN DE SEYP P. 182

editing, editen, edixyng: HENNIE FRANSSEN-SEEBREGTS

FOR ABRAMS
EDITOR: NATALIE KAIRE
DESIGNER: LIAM FLANAGAN
TRANSLATOR: MARLEEN REIMER
PRODUCTION MANAGER: ANET SIRNA-BRUDER

CATALOGING-IN-PUBLICATION DATA HAS BEEN APPLIED FOR AND MAY BE OBTAINED FROM THE LIBRARY OF CONGRESS.
ISBN 978-1-61769-015-0

©2012 YVETTE VAN BOVEN

ORIGINALLY PUBLISHED IN 2011 BY FONTAINE UITGEVERS
10 9 8 7 6 5 4 3 2

ALL RIGHTS RESERVED. NO PORTION OF THIS BOOK MAY BE REPRODUCED, STORED IN A RETRIEVAL SYSTEM, OR TRANSMITTED IN ANY FORM OR BY ANY MEANS, MECHANICAL, ELECTRONIC, PHOTOCOPYING, RECORDING, OR OTHERWISE, WITHOUT WRITTEN PERMISSION FROM THE PUBLISHER.

STEWART, TABORI & CHANG BOOKS ARE AVAILABLE AT SPECIAL DISCOUNTS WHEN PURCHASED IN QUANTITY FOR PREMIUMS AND PROMOTIONS AS WELL AS FUNDRAISING OR EDUCATIONAL USE. SPECIAL EDITIONS CAN ALSO BE CREATED TO SPECIFICATION. FOR DETAILS, CONTACT SPECIALSALES@ABRAMSBOOKS.COM OR THE ADDRESS BELOW.

ABRAMS
THE ART OF BOOKS SINCE 1949
115 WEST 18TH STREET
NEW YORK, NY 10011
WWW.ABRAMSBOOKS.COM

introduction

After a season full of travel, summer has finally arrived. My books now speak a lot of languages, and I am awfully proud of that. You'll often find me simply beaming, with rosy cheeks. You don't expect that from your books. I didn't raise them this way; they did it themselves. I wave to them like a proud mother every time they go off on a trip around the world, and sometimes I even go along—such fun!

But, I must say, one can get pretty tired of all that traveling, and that's why I'm glad summer is here. From my hammock I wave good-bye to my latest book with a large handkerchief. I'm excited about all the recipes it's going to bring to so many people, but I'm happy that now I—and you, too—can take it easy for a bit.

Summer offers so many fresh fruits and vegetables that there's almost no need to cook them: They are inherently tasty. And I know from experience that on hot summer days, few people are keen on spending long hours in the kitchen anyway.

That's why I wrote this book.

Her older sister, *Home Made Winter*, was filled with comfort-food recipes inspired by my childhood in cold, wet Ireland, with a nod to the Netherlands, my home, and France, my other home.

This *Summer* book is about my life now, in Amsterdam and Paris, but most of all it's about the summers my husband and I spend in Provence. From the time my husband was taking his first steps, he has spent his summers with family friends who own an orchard near Avignon. This family and Oof's family have known one another for generations, and now they have been friends with me for half my life.

The old Georges has taught me a lot. He takes me on walks and shows how they tie bottles to the blossoms on apple and pear trees, hoping they will bear fruit inside the bottle, which they can use to make liquor in the fall. Together we make jars of marmalade for the entire family and we create little labels for them. We inspect the beans and the artichokes in the vegetable garden.

We are lucky enough to accompany our friends to feasts at the neighbors' houses, and they teach us the region's customs. We host *grillades* (barbecues) in Norbert and Valerie's garden and watch the stars until deep in the night, drinking homemade spirits and generous glasses of wine from the village's cellar. Everybody prepares a part of the meal, so it's never much work for anyone in particular, which is nice.

That was the inspiration for how I organized my book.

Therefore I'm giving you recipes for dishes that usually don't take too much effort, and for dishes that essentially look after themselves. I've included ideas for long barbecue nights with family and friends, with lots of different side dishes, so everyone can make something and share the work. I'm giving you recipes for lots of festive summer drinks, too, so you can raise your glasses when I thank you for all the enthusiastic comments and cheerful reactions that I've received in the past months.

Thank you, and CHEERS!

To SUMMER!

Yvette

Wim Bijma's garden, Amsterdam

Near Marken

CONTENTS

Oof

BREAKFAST
BRUNCH
LUNCH

Italy

avocado, cucumber & lime shake

FOR 1 GLASS

½ avocado, peeled
⅓ cucumber, chopped
juice and zest of 1 lime
3 or 4 ice cubes
salt and freshly ground black pepper

Combine all the ingredients in a blender and puree. If you find the shake too thick, add some water.

frozen fruit smoothie

Like a liquid ice pop.

FOR 2 LARGE GLASSES

9 oz (250 g) mixed frozen fruit (or
    just one kind, like raspberries)
1 cup (200 ml) organic apple juice
1 tbsp chopped fresh tarragon

Combine all the ingredients in a blender and puree. Drink at once.

watermelon & yogurt smoothie

This smoothie isn't pictured, by the way.

FOR 4½ CUPS (1 L)

1 lb (500 g) watermelon, chopped
2 tbsp honey or date syrup
2 tbsp chopped fresh mint
17 oz (500 g) plain yogurt
1 tbsp cardamom pods, seeds
    ground in a mortar

Combine the watermelon, honey, and mint in a blender and puree. Add the yogurt and pulse a few times—briefly, or the smoothie will become too liquid.

Pour into glasses and sprinkle with the cardamom.

the ultimate "puffy" pancakes

If we have a hangover (which of course hardly ever happens), we make these pancakes in the late morning. I know: There are hundreds of recipes for pancakes . . . but this is truly the Ultimate Recipe. And you know I never lie.

FOR A BIG PILE OF 20 PANCAKES

2 cups (250 g) all-purpose flour
pinch of salt
1 tbsp plus 1 tsp (20 g) baking
    powder
1 tbsp sugar
2 tsp (1 envelope) vanilla sugar, or
    1 tsp vanilla extract
7 tbsp (100 g) butter, cut into
    chunks, plus more for the pan
1½ cups (350 ml) milk
2 large eggs, beaten

FOR SERVING
½ pint (200 g) raspberries
¾ cup (200 g) crème fraîche
superfine sugar for garnish

In a big bowl, combine the flour, salt, baking powder, and the plain and vanilla sugar (if using extract, add it later). Combine the butter and milk in a saucepan and heat over medium heat until the butter melts. Add the vanilla extract, if using.

Pour the warm milk-butter mixture into the flour mixture in the bowl while stirring, then whisk until all the lumps are dissolved.

Beat in the eggs.

Heat 1 teaspoon butter in a skillet over medium heat and pour three ladlefuls of batter into the pan, slightly apart so you have three small pancakes.

Cook for about 3 minutes, or until small holes break out on the surface, then flip and cook them for 2 minutes on the other side. Repeat with more butter and the remaining batter. Keep the cooked pancakes warm on a plate covered with foil in a low oven while you cook the rest.

Serve with raspberries, crème fraîche, and a sprinkle of superfine sugar.

STRAWBERRY SHORTCAKE

These cakelike scones are made in a snap and awfully delicious. I like to eat them with strawberries, though really they go nicely with any kind of fruit ♥

1½ PINTS (500 G) STRAWBERRIES, HULLED & HALVED

1 CUP SUGAR

GRATED ZEST OF 1 ORANGE

3½ CUPS (450 G) ALL-PURPOSE FLOUR

4 TSP BAKING POWDER

PINCH OF SALT

7 TBSP (100 G) COLD BUTTER (CUT INTO CHUNKS)

1 CUP (250 ML) HEAVY CREAM

2 LARGE EGGS

½ TSP VANILLA EXTRACT

PREHEAT THE OVEN TO 375°F (190°C). PUT THE STRAWBERRIES IN A BIG BOWL AND TOSS WITH ¼ CUP (50G) OF THE SUGAR AND THE ORANGE ZEST → LET STAND FOR 30 MINS.

IN A FOOD PROCESSOR, COMBINE THE FLOUR, BAKING POWDER, THE REMAINING ¾ CUP (150G) SUGAR & THE SALT → PULSE BRIEFLY TO COMBINE. THEN ADD THE BUTTER & PULSE TO INCORPORATE IT.

 IN A JUG WHISK ½ CUP (125 ML) OF THE CREAM WITH THE EGGS & VANILLA AND ADD THAT TO THE BUTTER-FLOUR MIXTURE

PULSE A FEW TIMES, UNTIL THE DOUGH JUST ABOUT STICKS TOGETHER.
➤➤ THE SECRET TO A TENDER & LIGHT CAKE IS KNOWING WHEN TO STOP MIXING (REALLY) ◄◄

WITH A WELL-GREASED SCOOP (I USE A MEASURING CUP), MAKE 6 BALLS FROM THE SLIGHTLY STICKY DOUGH. TAP YOUR SCOOP OR CUP ON A GREASED BAKING SHEET SO THE DOUGH FALLS OUT. → PLACE THE MOUNDS FAR APART: THEY'LL RISE A LOT!
BAKE THE SHORTCAKES FOR 12 TO 14 MINUTES, UNTIL GOLDEN. MEANWHILE, WHIP THE REMAINING CREAM UNTIL SOFT PEAKS FORM. LET THE SHORTCAKES COOL ON A RACK, THEN SPLIT THEM IN HALF & FILL WITH WHIPPED CREAM AND A GENEROUS SCOOP OF THE MACERATED STRAWBERRIES → AH!

making quark

It's a piece of cake. All you need is patience. If you use skim milk you'll get skim-milk quark; if you use whole milk you'll get whole-milk quark. Isn't life simple?

1. In a large saucepan, **combine** 6½ cups (1½ l) milk and 3 cups plus 2 tbsp (750 ml) buttermilk and warm over medium-low heat to 100°F (40°C). I check it with my meat thermometer, but if you don't have one then heat the milk until it's the temperature of hot bathwater and you see the milk begin to thicken. 2. **remove** the pan from the heat, cover it, and wrap it snugly in a towel. Place the pan in a warm spot for 24 hours, until the milk is thick. 3. **pour** the milk into a sieve lined with a clean lint-free towel or several layers of rinsed and squeezed cheesecloth and set the sieve over a bowl. Let it drain for a few hours. 4. Now you have at least 2 cups (500 g) quark. **keep** the quark in clean jars in the fridge.

cherry, blueberry, and/or blackberry jam with orange & basil

2 ¼ lb (1 kg) pitted cherries,
 blueberries, and/or blackberries
½ cup plus 2 tbsp (150 ml) orange
 juice
5 cups (1 kg) jam sugar, or 5 cups
 (1 kg) granulated sugar plus
 1 (1.75-ounce/50 g) envelope
 powdered pectin
1 small bunch of fresh basil (about
 ⅔ oz/20 g), stemmed

EXTRA:
4 to 6 half-pint jars, boiled for 10
 minutes and set on a clean
 dish towel

Combine all the ingredients except the basil in a large nonre-active pot and bring to a gentle boil over medium-high heat. Reduce the heat and simmer for about 20 minutes. Remove from the heat and puree the mixture with an immersion blender. Place 1 teaspoon of the jam on a saucer in the fridge for 10 minutes to see if it's thick enough. (It's up to you.)

If the jam isn't thick enough, put the pot back on the heat and simmer the mixture until it's the right consistency. Remove from the heat.

Add the basil leaves and puree the jam again. Immediately ladle the hot jam into the sterilized jars, screw the lids on, and turn the jars upside down. Let the jam cool upside down, then turn upright and store in the pantry. Serve on warm toast or stir into yogurt; keep opened jars in the refrigerator.

melon jam with tarragon

Make this jam with honeydew melon, cantaloupe, or galia—it's your choice (but don't use watermelon, which contains too much water). Tarragon is a nice addition (as you probably know by now, I like little surprises). And don't restrict this jam to toast; add a dollop to yogurt or a bowl of quark (page 16), or spoon it onto pancakes (page 13).

2 ¼ lb (1 kg) ripe melon, cleaned and
    chopped (about 2 small melons)
5 cups (1 kg) jam sugar, or
    5 cups (1 kg) sugar plus
    1 (1.75-ounce/50 g) envelope
    powdered pectin
1 orange
1 lemon
4 to 5 tbsp (about 15 g) finely
    chopped tarragon

EXTRA:

3 or 4 half-pint jars, boiled for
    10 minutes and set on a clean
    dish towel

Put the melon and sugar in a large nonreactive pot. Squeeze the orange and lemon and add the juice and squeezed-out rinds to the melon. Let the mixture macerate for at least 30 minutes, or preferably half a day.

Place the pan over high heat and bring to a boil, then reduce the heat to low and simmer for 5 minutes. Remove from the heat.

Place 1 teaspoon of the jam on a saucer in the fridge for 10 minutes. If it thickens nicely, the jam is done. If the jam is too liquid, simmer the mixture a bit longer. When the mixture reaches the desired consistency, remove the pot from the heat.

Remove the orange and lemon hulls from the pot and add the tarragon.

Use an immersion blender briefly to blend in the tarragon.

Immediately ladle the hot jam into the sterilized jars, screw the lids on, and turn the jars upside down. Let the jam cool upside down, then turn upright and store in the pantry. Store opened jars in the refrigerator.

easter

when we first moved to the netherlands we briefly
stayed in the southern province of limburg, until
my parents found a home in the city of haarlem in
northwest holland. this meant that for a while we
lived in a tiny village very close to my aunt and
uncle and a whole bunch of cousins.

to welcome us,
our family had
festively decorated
our entire house.
it was easter,
and limburgers
sure know how
to celebrate their
catholic holidays.

my sister and i didn't know where
to look first. what a sight! on the
table there was an enormous bunch
of flowering branches with easter eggs
dangling from them. i believe i found this
even more beautiful than a christmas
tree. it was unlike anything i'd ever seen. as
children in ireland we had been bombarded
with gigantic chocolate eggs, preferably
wrapped in colorful foil with plastic bows tied
around them, each egg containing a surprise. but the
tree of decorated easter eggs and other traditions were
all new to us.

we learned about easter egg hunts. we watched processions
go by: a pastor leading the way, followed by a real brass
band and troupes of baton–twirling majorettes. we carried palm
fronds and made rooster–shaped bread rolls to ornament them.

my mother told us to remember everything, because, she said, when
we move north you'll never experience anything like this again. she
was right, even though we dutifully painted our eggs every year.

23

marbled eggs with lavender salt

FOR THE EGGS
8 (free-range!) eggs
2 tbsp loose lapsang souchong tea,
    or 2 teabags

FOR THE SALT
3 tbsp coarse sea salt or flaky salt
1 tsp dried lavender (available in
    organic food stores)

Make the eggs: Bring a pot of water to a boil and add the eggs; boil for 8 minutes. Heat 4½ cups (1 l) water, add the tea leaves or bags, and make a pot of strong tea; let it steep for a while so that it becomes very dark, and leave the leaves or bags in it. After boiling the eggs, hold them under cold running water (it will make peeling easier later on), then roll them around on the counter to crack the shell without peeling the eggs.

Pour the tea (with the teabags or leaves still in it) into a wide bowl and submerge the cracked eggs in the tea. Put the bowl in the refrigerator for 24 hours.

Make the salt: Grind the salt and lavender in a mortar. Put it in a tiny serving bowl.

Take the eggs out of the tea and peel them. They will be nicely marbled and they'll have acquired a light smoky taste. Serve with the lavender salt.

fougasse provençale

A sweet bread.

5¼ cups (650 g) bread flour
¾ cup (150 g) superfine sugar
generous pinch of salt
2 (¼-oz/7-gm) envelopes active
    dry yeast
3 to 4 tbsp lukewarm water
2 eggs
grated zest and juice of 1 well-rinsed
    orange
⅓ cup plus 2 tbsp (100 ml) olive oil,
    plus more for brushing the loaves
1 tbsp orange blossom water
confectioners' sugar for garnish

Combine the flour, sugar, and salt in a large bowl. In a separate bowl, combine the yeast and the lukewarm water and let it dissolve. Make a well in the flour mixture and pour in the dissolved yeast. Dust some flour over the yeast mixture, then let it rest for about 15 minutes, or until it begins to foam a little. In a large measuring cup, whisk the eggs with the orange zest and juice, the oil, and the orange blossom water. You should have about 1½ cups (350 ml) liquid. Add some water if needed. Pour the egg mixture into the yeast mixture. Gently mix everything, then knead until you have a soft but not too sticky dough. If necessary, add more water or flour. Turn the dough out onto a well-floured counter and continue to knead for at least 10 minutes, until the dough is supple. Oil a baking sheet. Divide the dough into two or more equal parts (depending on the number of breads you'd like to bake), place them on the baking sheet, cover with a clean towel, and let rise for at least 1 hour, until doubled in volume. Roll out each of the dough balls on a floured countertop into a rectangular slab about 1 inch (2 cm) thick. With a knife, make a long straight cut all the way through the dough down the center of each rectangle, then make three short diagonal cuts on either side of the center cut—as if you were drawing the veins of a leaf. Carefully transfer the dough to the baking sheet, cover, and let rise for another 30 minutes. Preheat the oven to 350°F (180°C). Brush the loaves with some oil, then bake for 15 to 20 minutes, until the crust is crisp and nicely browned. Let cool on wire racks. Dust the top with confectioners' sugar, if you'd like.

fougasse with bacon and olives

A savory bread.

2 (¼-oz/7-gm) envelopes active
    dry yeast
1¼ cups (300 ml) lukewarm water
4 cups (500 g) bread flour
1 tbsp salt
3 tbsp olive oil, plus extra for
    brushing the loaves
5 oz (150 g) bacon, diced
3½ oz (100 g) black olives, pitted,
    sliced into rings
handful of fresh herbs, chopped:
    rosemary, thyme, whatever you
    have around
Coarse salt or grated hard cheese
    (optional)

Dissolve the yeast in about 3 tbsp of the lukewarm water. Put the flour in a large bowl and add the dissolved yeast, the regular salt, the remaining water, and the oil. Knead everything into a firm ball of dough. Turn the dough out onto a well-floured counter and continue kneading. Don't rush. It will take at least 10 minutes before you get a nice firm dough that won't stick. Fry the bacon in a skillet over low heat (so you won't need to use any fat). Remove to paper towels to cool completely, then knead the bacon pieces into the dough, along with the olives and herbs. Oil a baking sheet. Divide the dough into two or more equal parts (all depends on the number of breads you'd like to bake), place them on the baking sheet, cover with a clean towel, and let them rise for at least 1½ hours, until doubled in volume. Roll out each of the dough balls on a floured countertop into a rectangular slab about 1 inch (2 cm) thick. With a knife, make a long straight cut all the way through the dough down the center of each rectangle, then make three short diagonal cuts on either side of the center cut—as if you were drawing the veins of a leaf. Carefully transfer the dough to the baking sheet, cover, and let rise for another 30 minutes. Preheat the oven to 350°F (180°C). Brush the loaves with some oil, and sprinkle with coarse salt or cheese if you like. Bake for about 25 minutes (depending on the size of the loaves), until the crust is crisp and nicely browned. Let cool on wire racks.

herb salad from the garden with a poached egg

This simple salad demands some preparation, so I wrote the recipe down in a way that should enable you to prepare it an evening in advance. The result is so good that it's absolutely worth the effort . . . so do try it.

FOR THE EGGS
splash of vinegar
4 large cage-free eggs, as fresh as
   possible

FOR THE HOLLANDAISE SAUCE
2 large egg yolks
1 tbsp prepared green herb mustard
   (Maille brand is good)
2 tbsp white wine vinegar or lemon
   juice
1 cup plus 2 tbsp (250 g) good-
   quality unsalted butter, cut into
   small cubes
2 tbsp chopped fresh tarragon

FOR THE SALAD
1 head of curly lettuce, or any other
   nice light green lettuce, inner
   light green leaves only
1 large bunch of herbs, such as
   chervil, chives, or dill (at least
   3½ oz/100 g)
edible flowers from the garden:
   borage, mint flowers, Japanese
   cherry blossoms, daisies,
   whatever you have (they're not
   essential, but they're pretty)
1 small baguette, cut on a sharp
   diagonal into slices and toasted

Poach the eggs: Bring a medium saucepan of water to a boil and add a splash of vinegar to the water. Gently break an egg into a sieve. Gently shake the sieve to enable the watery part of the egg white to drain out (when using older eggs there will be more moisture then when using fresh eggs). Keep the water near boiling and stir it to make a little whirlpool in the pan. Slide the egg into the water. Poach for 2 to 3 minutes, then scoop the egg out of the pan with a skimmer. Transfer the egg to a warm plate and cover it loosely with aluminum foil. Repeat with the remaining eggs. If you prepare the eggs in advance, slide them gently into a bowl, cover with cool water, add a dash of vinegar, and refrigerate them for up to 1 day.

Make the hollandaise sauce: Bring a double boiler or saucepan with 1 inch of water to a boil. In the top of the boiler or in a metal bowl that fits on top of the pan, combine the egg yolks, mustard, vinegar, and 2 tbsp water. Place the pan or bowl on top of the boiler, making sure the boiling water doesn't touch the bottom of the bowl (this technique is called *au bain marie*). Lower the heat so the water is just at a simmer and use a whisk or a hand mixer to whisk the mixture constantly for 5 to 10 minutes, until it turns into a nice, firm foam. Don't stop whisking or the eggs will set at the bottom and you'll have to start all over again. Keep whisking while adding the butter a piece at a time. Add the next cube only after the previous one has melted. You are looking for a mayonnaise-like sauce. If the sauce is too thick, you can add a few drops of boiling water. Finish by mixing in the tarragon.

Remove the pan or bowl from the water and cover it with a lid or plate for a few minutes until serving. You can easily make the sauce half a day in advance and store it in a squeaky-clean Thermos at room temperature; hollandaise should always be served lukewarm. Don't try to reheat the sauce, or it will curdle and you'll have to start over.

Make the salad: Wash the lettuce, herbs, and flowers and dry them in a salad spinner. If you poached the eggs in advance, heat a saucepan of water to near boiling. Add the poached eggs and rewarm them for no longer than 2 minutes. Arrange the salad over 4 plates. Place the poached eggs on top. Pour hollandaise sauce over the eggs and place a long, pretty baguette toast alongside.

Schellingwoude, Amsterdam

Wim Bijma's greenhouse, Amsterdam

carrot pie with apple and goat cheese

Make this.

FOR 6 TO 8 SERVINGS

8 carrots, peeled
1 sheet frozen puff pastry, thawed
1 onion, halved lengthwise and
    thinly sliced
1 fresh, tart apple, peeled, cored, and
    sliced as thinly as possible
4 oz (100 g) soft goat cheese
½ cup (100 g) crème fraîche
½ cup plus 2 tbsp (150 ml) carrot
    juice
3 large eggs
salt and freshly ground black pepper

Boil the carrots in salted water for 8 minutes, until just tender. Drain and rinse under cold running water. Halve them lengthwise and set them aside.

Grease a 9-inch (24-cm) tart pan with a removable bottom with a little butter.

On a well-floured counter, roll out the puff pastry into a nice round slab the size of the pie plate. Press the dough firmly into the plate and trim the edges neatly. With a fork, stab some holes in the bottom, then cover the dough and place the pie plate in the fridge for 30 minutes.

Preheat the oven to 350°F (180°C).

Arrange the onion and apple over the bottom of the pastry in the pie plate and place the halved carrots on top in a spoke pattern. Crumble the goat cheese over the pie, somewhat in between the carrots.

In a medium bowl, whisk together the crème fraîche, carrot juice, and eggs. Season with salt and pepper. Pour the mixture over the carrots and sprinkle everything generously with pepper.

Bake the pie on the lower rack of the oven for about 35 minutes, until golden brown.

ASPARAGUS PIE

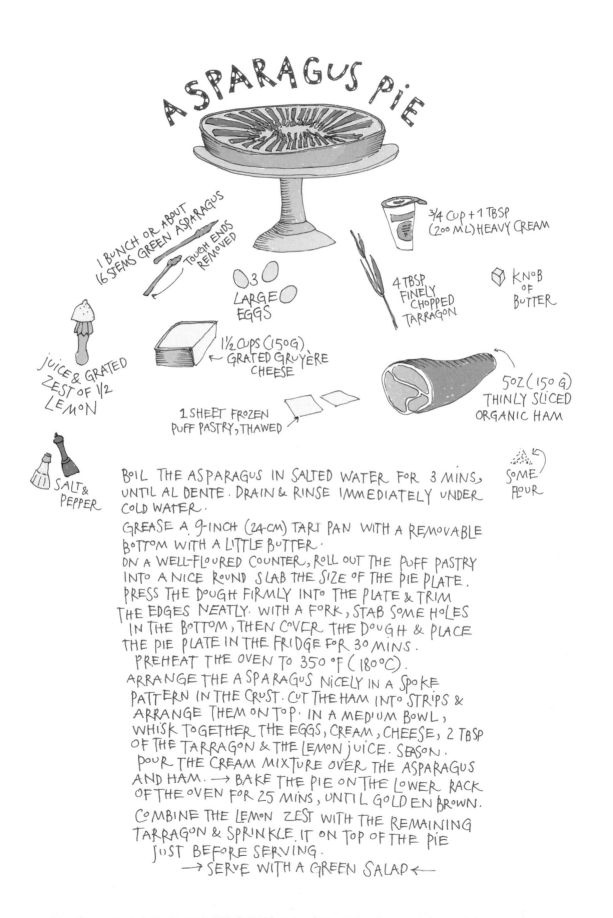

1 BUNCH OR ABOUT 16 STEMS GREEN ASPARAGUS, TOUGH ENDS REMOVED

3 LARGE EGGS

3/4 CUP + 1 TBSP (200 ML) HEAVY CREAM

4 TBSP FINELY CHOPPED TARRAGON

KNOB OF BUTTER

JUICE & GRATED ZEST OF 1/2 LEMON

1 1/2 CUPS (150 G) GRATED GRUYÈRE CHEESE

5 OZ (150 G) THINLY SLICED ORGANIC HAM

1 SHEET FROZEN PUFF PASTRY, THAWED

SALT & PEPPER

SOME FLOUR

BOIL THE ASPARAGUS IN SALTED WATER FOR 3 MINS, UNTIL AL DENTE. DRAIN & RINSE IMMEDIATELY UNDER COLD WATER.

GREASE A 9-INCH (24-CM) TART PAN WITH A REMOVABLE BOTTOM WITH A LITTLE BUTTER.

ON A WELL-FLOURED COUNTER, ROLL OUT THE PUFF PASTRY INTO A NICE ROUND SLAB THE SIZE OF THE PIE PLATE. PRESS THE DOUGH FIRMLY INTO THE PLATE & TRIM THE EDGES NEATLY. WITH A FORK, STAB SOME HOLES IN THE BOTTOM, THEN COVER THE DOUGH & PLACE THE PIE PLATE IN THE FRIDGE FOR 30 MINS.

PREHEAT THE OVEN TO 350°F (180°C).

ARRANGE THE ASPARAGUS NICELY IN A SPOKE PATTERN IN THE CRUST. CUT THE HAM INTO STRIPS & ARRANGE THEM ON TOP. IN A MEDIUM BOWL, WHISK TOGETHER THE EGGS, CREAM, CHEESE, 2 TBSP OF THE TARRAGON & THE LEMON JUICE. SEASON.

POUR THE CREAM MIXTURE OVER THE ASPARAGUS AND HAM. → BAKE THE PIE ON THE LOWER RACK OF THE OVEN FOR 25 MINS, UNTIL GOLDEN BROWN.

COMBINE THE LEMON ZEST WITH THE REMAINING TARRAGON & SPRINKLE IT ON TOP OF THE PIE JUST BEFORE SERVING.

→ SERVE WITH A GREEN SALAD ←

rolled–up spinach omelet with creamy filling of goat cheese and dried tomato

FOR 8 TO 10 SERVINGS

FOR THE DRIED TOMATOES
about 30 tasty cherry tomatoes
pinch of salt and freshly ground
    black pepper
1 tbsp fresh oregano
2 cloves garlic, minced
olive oil

AND IF YOU WISH TO PRESERVE THEM:
about 1 cup (250 ml) light olive oil
    and a clean jar with a lid

FOR THE OMELET
14 oz (400 g) cleaned spinach
5 large eggs, separated
3 tbsp self-rising flour
⅔ cup (150 g) plus 1 tbsp quark
    (page 16)
salt and freshly ground black pepper
4 oz (100 g) cream cheese
4 oz (100 g) soft goat cheese
a handful of fresh herbs: tarragon,
    chervil, and chives, for example

Make the dried tomatoes: Preheat the oven to 250°F (120°C). Halve the tomatoes and place them on a baking sheet. Sprinkle with the salt, pepper, oregano, and garlic and trickle some olive oil over them. Bake for 2½ hours, then let them cool.

You can now use them in a recipe or preserve them in a clean jar. To preserve them, put them in the jar and pour oil on top until they are completely covered. Tap the jar lightly against the countertop to remove any air pockets. Keep in the fridge.

Make the omelet: Preheat the oven to 350°F (180°C). Line a 12-by-16-inch (30-by-40-cm) baking sheet with parchment paper.

Bring a large pot of water to a boil and blanch the spinach briefly. Use a skimmer to scoop the spinach out of the pan and drain it thoroughly in a strainer. Press the spinach firmly with the back of the skimmer.

Put the squeezed-out spinach in a food processor and add the egg yolks, flour, and 1 tbsp quark. Season with salt and pepper. Pulse the mixture until smooth.

In a separate, very clean, large bowl beat the egg whites with a pinch of salt until stiff. Fold in the spinach mixture. With a knife, spread the batter over the baking sheet and bake the omelet in the middle of the oven for 12 to 15 minutes, or until the egg feels firm to the touch.

In the meantime, in a medium bowl, beat the remaining quark with the cream cheese and goat cheese until smooth. Finely chop all the herbs and stir them in.

Place a sheet of parchment on the counter. Invert the omelet onto the parchment and gently peel the parchment from the back of the omelet.

Spread the cheese mixture over the omelet and sprinkle a few handfuls of the tomatoes on top.

Roll up the omelet tightly, using the bottom parchment sheet to help you. Place the roll in the fridge for at least 1 hour to firm up.

Cut into slices with a thin, sharp knife. Serve with crisp toast.

SAVORY CAKES

These two cakes are very different, the first one crumbly and spicy, the other moist and rich, almost a meal in itself. Serve a slice or two with soup or a salad, or eat them just as they are, with a glass of cool wine at the end of the day.

arugula cake with pine nuts

3½ oz (100 g) arugula (parsley or
    spinach is also an option)
1½ cups (175 g) self-rising flour
3 large eggs
2 tbsp sour cream
4 tbsp olive oil
1 generous tbsp prepared mustard
salt and freshly ground black pepper
½ cup (50 g) pine nuts

Preheat the oven to 325°F (160°C). Generously grease a 5-by-9-inch (1-l) loaf pan.

Rinse the arugula, dry it in a salad spinner or in a dishcloth, and chop it.

In a large bowl, combine the flour, eggs, sour cream, oil, and mustard. Season with salt and pepper. Using an electric mixer, beat at the highest speed for 1 minute to combine thoroughly.

Fold in the arugula and pine nuts.

Pour the batter into the prepared pan and bake for 40 minutes, or until a skewer inserted in the center comes out clean.

Let the cake cool for 5 minutes, then turn it out of the pan.

Serve warm or at room temperature. Store in the refrigerator, wrapped.

feta & olive cake

I was given this recipe by the brother of my sister's husband (are you still with me?). It's delicious, and that's why I'm passing it on to you, with love. Substitute to taste: finely chopped fresh or roasted bell peppers instead of olives, or blue cheese instead of feta, for example.

1¾ cups (225 g) self-rising flour
⅓ cup plus 2 tbsp (100 ml) olive oil
⅓ cup plus 2 tbsp (100 ml) white
    wine
3 large eggs
1 cup (100 g) grated Parmesan
    cheese
salt and freshly ground black pepper
5 oz (150 g) feta, diced
9 oz (250 g) mixed olives, pitted

Preheat the oven to 325°F (160°C). Generously grease a 5-by-9-inch (1-l) loaf pan.

In a large bowl, combine the flour, oil, wine, eggs, and Parmesan and whisk until smooth. Season with salt and pepper and stir in the feta and olives.

Pour the mixture into the prepared pan and bake for about 45 minutes, or until a skewer inserted in the center comes out clean.

Let the cake cool for 5 minutes, then turn it out of the pan.

Serve warm or at room temperature. Store in the refrigerator, wrapped.

WONTON RAVIOLI WITH RICOTTA
⋙→ FOR 2 ←⋘

FIRST MAKE THE FILLING:

mix:

1 CUP + 1 TBSP (250 G) RICOTTA

1 EGG

2 TBSP. GRATED PARMESAN CHEESE

SALT & PEPPER

+ 1 TBSP CHOPPED FLAT-LEAF PARSLEY

THAW 1 PACKAGE OF FROZEN WONTON SHEETS. (AVAILABLE IN SPECIALTY STORES!)

place: 12 SHEETS ON THE COUNTER.

PLACE 1 TSP OF THE RICOTTA MIXTURE IN THE CENTER OF EACH

→ WET THE EDGES WITH A BRUSH

& PLACE ANOTHER SHEET ON TOP. FIRMLY PRESS THE EDGES TOGETHER!

BOIL 4-5 RAVIOLI AT ONCE IN A LARGE PAN OF SALTED WATER FOR 3-4 MINS, UNTIL JUST TENDER.

whisk: A SAUCE OF:

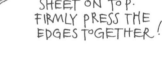

2 TBSP OLIVE OIL
2 TBSP LEMON JUICE
4 TBSP HOT CHICKEN BROTH
SALT & PEPPER

POUR THE SAUCE OVER THE HOT RAVIOLI → ENJOY.

lebanese bread salad–fattoush

I can live on this salad alone. Don't skimp on the herbs, the more the better.

FOR THE SALAD
2 eggplants, diced
4 shallots, peeled and quartered
1 or 2 cloves garlic, pushed through a
    garlic press
splash of olive oil
salt and freshly ground black pepper
4 pita breads, split horizontally in half
9 oz (250 g) sweet cherry tomatoes
1 small cucumber, diced
a generous handful of fresh mint
    leaves, coarsely chopped
a generous handful of fresh flat-leaf
    parsley, coarsely chopped
3 oz (75 g) kalamata olives, pitted
    (or other nice olives, taggiasche,
    for example)
seeds of ½ pomegranate

FOR THE DRESSING
⅓ cup (75 ml) red wine vinegar
1 tsp sumac (this is a tart red
    powder from the drupes of
    a Sumac shrub, available in
    Middle Eastern grocery stores;
    substitute 1 tbsp lemon juice)
1 tbsp harissa, or to taste
2 tbsp honey
½ cup plus 2 tbsp (150 ml) extra-
    virgin olive oil

Preheat the oven to 350°F (180°C).

Make the salad: In a bowl, combine the eggplants, shallots, and garlic. Pour some oil over it and sprinkle with salt and pepper. Spread the mixture out over a baking sheet in a single layer or it won't roast well. Roast the eggplant mixture for 25 minutes, or until light brown. Spoon the eggplant mixture into a large bowl.

Place the pita breads on the baking sheet and brush them with oil. Bake for 10 minutes, until lightly browned, and then flip them and bake for another 5 minutes. Let them cool and break them into pieces.

Make the dressing: In a small bowl, whisk together the vinegar, sumac, harissa, and honey. Trickle in the oil and beat until you have a smooth dressing.

To the bowl of eggplant, add the tomatoes, cucumber, herbs, olives, and pomegranate seeds. Add the dressing and toss.

Garnish the salad with pieces of pita and serve with labneh.

spicy labneh

1 clove garlic, pushed through a
    garlic press
½ tsp salt
1 tsp paprika
4½ cups (1 kg) plain yogurt
a generous handful of fresh herbs,
    coarsely chopped: parsley, mint,
    cilantro, and dill
a few drops of extra-virgin olive oil
1 tbsp cumin seed, toasted briefly in
    a dry skillet
and perhaps some red pepper flakes
    (to taste)

In a medium bowl, stir the garlic, salt, and paprika into the yogurt.

Place a clean dish towel in a strainer and pour in the seasoned yogurt. Make a knot in the towel and hang the bundle of yogurt above a bucket or over the sink. The longer you let it drain, the firmer your labneh will be. (If you drain it for longer than 1 day, move it to the refrigerator.)

Thoroughly stir the yogurt and spoon it into a big bowl. Sprinkle it with the chopped herbs and trickle some oil over it, then the toasted cumin seeds and red pepper flakes.

Slice toasted pita bread into strips and serve. You can also eat labneh on bread, with radishes as a snack, or with the salad above.

With Carrie and Little Marie

"tarte d'abricots" with orange blossom and honey

A somewhat elaborate pie, but the result justifies the effort, so it's okay.

In the Provence region there's usually an abundance of apricots in summer, and Georges will sometimes, quietly, while we're still sleeping, leave a handful of apricots on our breakfast table after he bikes his morning rounds in the orchard.

FOR THE DOUGH

1 cup (125 g) all-purpose flour
½ cup (75 g) almond flour (from the
    organic store) or finely ground
    almonds
¼ cup (50 g) superfine sugar
pinch of salt
9 tbsp (125 g) cold unsalted butter
ice-cold water

FOR THE FILLING

½ cup plus 2 tbsp (150 ml) whole
    milk
1 vanilla bean, split and seeds
    scraped
2 large egg yolks, plus 1 whole egg
3 tbsp honey
1 tbsp cornstarch
¾ cup (125 g) whole blanched
    almonds
½ cup (60 g) confectioners' sugar
3 tbsp (50 g) unsalted butter, at
    room temperature
pinch of salt
1 tsp orange blossom water
about 10 fresh apricots, halved and
    pitted

TO GARNISH

3 tbsp sliced almonds, lightly toasted
    in a dry skillet
3 tbsp honey

Make the dough: In the bowl of a food processor, combine the flours, sugar, and salt, and pulse briefly to combine. Add the cold butter and pulse to combine. Add a few drops of ice-cold water until the dough just sticks together. Don't process for too long, or the dough will become tough; you want it nice and crumbly. Form a flat round slab with dough and wrap in plastic. Refrigerate for at least 1 hour or up to 1 day.

Make the filling: In a small saucepan over medium-high heat, combine the milk with the vanilla seeds and bean and bring almost to a boil. Reduce the heat to low and let the mixture steep for 10 minutes. Remove from the heat.

In a large bowl, beat the egg yolks and whole egg with the honey and cornstarch until foamy. Remove the vanilla bean from the milk and pour the warm milk into the egg mixture while stirring, then pour the mixture back into the saucepan. Stir constantly over medium heat for about 10 minutes, until the custard thickens. Pour the custard into a clean bowl to let it cool completely.

Preheat the oven to 350°F (180°C). Butter a shallow 9-inch (24-cm) tart pan.

Roll out the dough on a floured counter and fit it into the pan. Trim the edges and prick a few holes in the bottom with a fork. Place the crust in the freezer for 20 minutes.

Bake the crust for about 20 minutes, until light brown. Let it cool on a rack. Leave the oven on.

In a food processor, grind the blanched almonds with the confectioners' sugar into a coarse powder. Pour in the custard and add the soft butter, salt, and orange blossom water and pulse to combine.

Pour the custard into the prebaked crust. Arrange the apricot halves over it, pitted side down. Bake the tart on a rack just below the center of the oven for 20 to 25 minutes, until golden brown.

Serve at room temperature, sprinkled with the sliced almonds and drizzled with honey.

cake with raspberries, blueberries, and coconut

This cake is an ode to rolled oats. The Irish (and the English) have known for a long time that adding oats to a batter makes cookies and cakes nicely crumbly and crunchy, but the Dutch have yet to learn that. You don't even find rolled oats among the baking products; you need to march on, a few aisles down, to the cereals. Buy a box; you'll use it often, for the flapjacks in my Winter book, for example. Or for this cake.

2 cups (250 g) self-rising flour
⅔ cup (50 g) rolled oats
1¼ cups (275 g) packed light brown sugar
pinch of salt
¾ cup (75 g) sweetened flaked coconut
½ cup plus 6 tbsp (200 g) cold butter, cut into small chunks
2 large eggs, beaten
1½ pints (500 g) fresh summer berries, such as raspberries and blueberries
confectioners' sugar

Preheat the oven to 350°F (180°C). Line the bottom of a 9-inch (23-cm) square baking pan with parchment paper and butter the paper.

Combine the flour, oats, brown sugar, salt, and coconut in the bowl of a food processor and add the cold butter. Pulse into a crumbly dough. (You can also do this by hand, but then work swiftly and with cold hands.)

Set 1¾ cups (200 g) of this mixture aside in a small bowl. Add the eggs to the mixture in the larger bowl and pulse until combined.

Press the dough containing the eggs into the prepared baking pan and smooth it with the wetted back of a spoon.

Arrange the berries on the dough. Sprinkle the entire cake with the 1¾ cups (200 g) of crumbly dough that you set aside.

Bake for 35 to 40 minutes, until a skewer inserted in the center comes out clean and the top is a nice golden brown.

Let the cake cool and cut into squares. Sprinkle with confectioners' sugar to serve.

The cake will keep in an airtight container for up to 1 week.

rhubarb pie with almond paste

Rhubarb: You could wake me up for that in the middle of the night. Delicious. Especially in this pie. With almond paste, nuts, and orange zest . . . mmmm!

FOR THE FILLING

1¼ lb (600 g) rhubarb, cut into
    ½-inch (1.5-cm) pieces
1 cup plus 2 tbsp (250 g) packed
    light brown sugar
1 tbsp ground cinnamon
1 tsp freshly grated nutmeg
seeds from 1 vanilla bean
grated zest of 1 orange
juice of ½ orange
½ cup (50 g) hazelnuts
5 oz (150 g) almond paste

FOR THE DOUGH

3¼ cups (400 g) all-purpose flour,
    plus more if needed
1 tsp baking powder
pinch of salt
½ cup plus 2 tbsp (125 g) sugar
9 tbsp (125 g) cold butter, plus more
    for greasing
about ⅓ cup (70 ml) milk
2 large eggs (1 separated)

Butter a deep 9-inch (24-cm) tart pan.

Make the filling: In a large bowl, combine the rhubarb, brown sugar, cinnamon, nutmeg, vanilla seeds, orange zest and juice, and hazelnuts. Set the mixture aside to macerate, tossing occasionally.

Make the dough: In a large bowl, combine the flour, baking powder, salt, and sugar. With cool hands or in a food processor, swiftly work in the cold butter, until the dough resembles coarse crumbs.

In a second bowl, whisk together the milk, whole egg, and egg yolk.

Make a depression in the middle of the flour mixture and pour in the milk mixture. Stir with a wooden spatula until you have a nice soft dough that's not sticky. You may need a bit more flour.

Divide the dough in two equal parts, wrap them in plastic, and refrigerate for 1 hour to stiffen.

Preheat the oven to 350°F (175°C).

Roll out one ball of dough on a well-floured counter. The dough will be pretty soft, so while rolling, you'll need to sprinkle more flour over the rolling pin and the dough.

Fit the dough into the pie plate and neatly trim the edges. Crumble the almond paste over the bottom and spread it evenly.

Spoon all the rhubarb from the bowl into the crust. If there is a lot of liquid in the bowl, leave it behind, or the bottom of the pie will become soggy.

Roll out the other ball of dough and place it over the pie. With a fork, press the edges firmly together. With an apple corer or knife, cut a hole in the center to allow steam to escape from the pie.

Beat the remaining egg white and brush the entire pie with it.

Bake in the center of the oven for 35 to 45 minutes, until golden brown. Let the pie cool, then serve it warm or at room temperature with whipped cream.

peach tart

This ridiculously simple tart is as easy as one, two, three. I like to use peaches, but you can make it with practically any type of fruit. Think: nectarines, apples, pears, apricots . . . whatever you happen to have lying around in your fruit bowl. Serve with lightly sweetened whipped cream or crème fraîche.

FOR THE DOUGH
1½ cups (175 g) all-purpose flour
pinch of salt
1 tbsp sugar
9 tbsp (125 g) cold butter, cut into
  chunks
about 3 tbsp ice-cold water

FOR THE FILLING
3 or 4 fresh ripe peaches
pinch of salt
3 to 4 tbsp sugar

Make the dough: It's easiest in a food processor, but by hand is fine as long as you knead swiftly with cold hands. Combine the flour, salt, and sugar. Add the butter and pulse to combine. Add drops of water until the dough just sticks together. Form a disk, wrap it in plastic, and leave it in the fridge to rest for at least 30 minutes.

Make the filling: Halve and pit the peaches and slice them. In a large bowl, sprinkle the peaches with a pinch of salt and the sugar. Let them rest for a half hour or so.

Preheat the oven to 400°F (200°C). Line a baking sheet with parchment.

Take the dough out of the fridge and roll it out on a floured counter to a rough circle about 10 to 12 inches (25 to 30 cm) in diameter. Transfer the dough to the lined baking sheet.

Pile the fruit in the center of the dough, leaving about a 1½-inch (4-cm) margin all around the edges. Fold the edges in over the fruit. (This edge doesn't have to be perfectly even. A little imperfection adds character. It's called *Home Made*.)

Bake for about 35 minutes, until golden brown.

Eat the tart while still warm, sprinkled with some extra sugar and dolloped with whipped cream— whisked by hand!— or vanilla ice cream.

macarons

1. grind 1¾ cups (175 g) confectioners' sugar with ¾ cup (100 g) almond flour in a processor until it's super fine, then sift it in a medium-mesh sieve. **2. separate** 3 eggs and keep the whites in a bowl for 3 days in the fridge. In a clean bowl, whisk three-day-old egg whites (100 g) until soft peaks form, then bit by bit, pour in 2 tbsp (25 g) superfine sugar while whisking. **3. add** the almond mixture to the egg whites and carefully fold it in so that it blends nicely. If you wish, you can add a drop of food coloring. **4. fill** a pastry bag with the mixture and pipe small rounds of the dough (about 1 inch/2 cm in diameter) on a parchment paper–lined baking sheet. **5.** If it's easier, you can first use a small glass to **draw** little circles on the parchment

paper as a guide. Don't fill the circles entirely, as the macarons will expand a little. **6.** let the macarons **rest** for 45 minutes to 1 hour, so they acquire a nice "skin." When they lose their gloss, it's time to bake them. **7.** **preheat** the oven to 300°F (150°C) and bake the macarons for 10 to 20 minutes (depending on their size). Keep a sharp eye on the oven temperature. I use an oven thermometer, as often the actual heat doesn't coincide with what you've set the temperature to. **8.** **during** the baking process the macarons get their typical "feet" at the base. They are ready when the tops first start to feel firm. Let them cool completely before filling and sandwiching them.

super macarons with raspberries and pink mascarpone

FOR THE FILLING
1 cup plus 1 tbsp (250 g)
    mascarpone
3 tbsp heavy cream
2 to 3 tbsp superfine sugar
seeds from 1 vanilla bean
2 tbsp (*Home Made*) raspberry jam
1 pint (300 g) raspberries

FOR 6 MACARONS
12 large (2¾- to 3 ¼-inch / 7- to
    8-cm) macaron shells (see
    recipe on pages 54–55)

Make the filling: In a medium bowl, use a whisk to combine the mascarpone with the cream, sugar, and vanilla bean seeds. Gently fold in the raspberry jam and then half of the fresh raspberries and stir until you have a creamy, rough filling.

Place a spoonful of cream on the flat side of one macaron shell, arrange about 5 raspberries on the filling, and press another macaron shell on top. Serve immediately.

You could also make this with apricot jam and fresh apricots, or the apricots in muscat syrup on page 238.

other fillings:

The lemon crème and pink grapefruit crème on page 222.

The lavender crème from the éclairs on page 70 (if you want, you can replace the lavender with something else: mint, instant coffee, allspice, anything you can come up with).

Charles & Matthis

Piedmont, Italy

58

banana crumble muffins

FOR THE BATTER: 3 BANANAS • 3/4 CUP (150 G) SUGAR • 1 LARGE EGG, BEATEN •
5 TBSP (75 G) UNSALTED BUTTER, MELTED • 1 2/3 CUPS (200 G) SELF-RISING FLOUR • PINCH OF SALT

FOR THE CRUMBLE: 1/3 CUP (75 G) PACKED BROWN SUGAR •
1 TBSP ALL-PURPOSE FLOUR • 1 TSP CINNAMON • 1 TBSP UNSALTED BUTTER

PREHEAT THE OVEN TO 350°F (180°C).

MAKE THE BATTER: MASH THE BANANAS IN A LARGE BOWL AND ADD THE SUGAR, EGG,
AND MELTED BUTTER. BEAT TO MAKE AN AIRY BATTER. (I USE A FOOD PROCESSOR BUT
A HAND MIXER WORKS EQUALLY WELL.) GENTLY STIR IN THE FLOUR AND SALT.

POUR THE BATTER INTO 12 GREASED OR LINED MUFFIN TIN CUPS.

MAKE THE CRUMBLE: IN A SMALL BOWL, SWIFTLY COMBINE ALL THE INGREDIENTS INTO A CRUMBLY MIXTURE.
SPRINKLE SOME CRUMBLE ON TOP OF EACH MUFFIN AND BAKE FOR ABOUT 17 MINUTES, UNTIL GOLDEN BROWN.

EAT PLAIN, FOR BRUNCH ON A LAZY SUNDAY, OR WARM WITH VANILLA ICE CREAM FOR DESSERT.

a summery cake with lemongrass syrup

FOR THE CAKE
½ tsp baking powder
pinch of salt
1½ cups (175 g) self-rising flour
¾ cup (175 g) unsalted butter, at
    room temperature
½ cup plus 2 tbsp (125 g) superfine
    sugar
3 large eggs
grated zest of 1 lemon

FOR THE SYRUP
1 cup (200 g) sugar
3 stalks of fresh lemongrass, cut into
    chunks

Make the cake: Preheat the oven to 350°F (170°C). Grease a 4-cup (1-l) Bundt pan or other cake pan.

Sift the baking powder, salt, and flour together into a small bowl. In a large bowl, beat the butter with the sugar until it's creamy and white. Add the eggs one by one, beating after each addition, then beat in the lemon zest and the flour in two or three parts until well combined. Pour the batter into the prepared cake pan and bake for 35 to 40 minutes, until a skewer inserted in the center comes out clean. Let the cake cool for 5 minutes, then invert it onto a plate to let it cool further.

While the cake is baking, make the syrup: In a medium saucepan over medium-high heat, bring ¾ cup (200 ml) water, the sugar, and the lemongrass to a simmer. Reduce the heat to low and let the mixture steep for about 20 minutes. Strain the syrup into a pitcher and throw out the lemongrass.

Pour one third of the syrup on top of the cake just after you've removed it from the pan, and let it soak in. Then take your time pouring the rest of the syrup over the cake, say a splash every time you walk by. Continue until all the syrup is absorbed. Store the cake at room temperature, covered with plastic wrap.

coconut & lime cheesecake

FOR THE CRUST

1 package of amaretti cookies (about
    7 oz / 200 g)
5 tbsp (75 g) unsalted butter, melted,
    plus more for greasing
pinch of salt

FOR THE FILLING

14 oz (400 g) cream cheese, at room
    temperature
2 cups plus 2 tbsp (500 g) quark
    (page 16)
1 can of unsweetened coconut milk
    (13.5 oz / 400 ml)
1¼ cups (250 g) sugar
grated zest and juice of 2 limes
pinch of salt
6 large eggs

FOR GARNISH

1 fresh coconut

Preheat the oven to 350°F (180°C). Butter a 9-inch (24-cm) springform pan. Line the bottom with parchment paper and butter the paper.

Make the crust: In a food processor, grind the cookies into fine crumbs. Add the melted butter and salt, and pulse until combined. Press the crumbly mixture into the bottom and ½ inch (1 cm) up the sides of the prepared pan. Bake for 12 to 15 minutes, then let the crust cool on a rack.

Lower the oven temperature to 325°F (160°C).

Make the filling: In a large bowl using an electric mixer, beat the cream cheese until creamy. Beat in the quark and the coconut milk. Add the sugar bit by bit, then stir in half of the lime zest and all the juice and the salt. Add the eggs one at a time and beat to combine. Pour the filling into the prebaked crust.

Bake about 1½ hours, until the center of the cake is just about firm.

Let cool for 20 minutes in the pan, then slide a knife around the edge of the pan to loosen the cake, to prevent it from cracking as it cools.

Let the cheesecake cool completely.

Cover the cake with aluminum foil and refrigerate at least overnight.

Now you can garnish it.

Open the coconut: With hammer and nail, penetrate two of its three eyes (the dark spots on top of the coconut). Through one of the holes, pour the coconut water out into a bowl.

Place the coconut on a firm base (outside on your stoop, for example) wrapped tightly in a dishcloth and hit it with a hammer until it breaks.

With a sharp knife, cut the meat out of the coconut. You can peel off the brown skin with a vegetable peeler, but I think it's prettier to leave it on. You can now use a peeler to slice strips and curls of coconut to garnish the cake, or you could grate it.

Remove the sides of the springform pan and place the cake on a platter. Garnish the top with the coconut curls and the rest of the lime zest.

zucchini cake with lemon glaze

If you've ever had a vegetable garden, you've probably experienced this phenomenon: zucchinis that never stop producing.

At the end of summer I didn't have a clue what to do with them anymore: zucchini cookies (recipe in **Home Made***), zucchini soup, savory pies (*Home Made Winter*), on pizza (also in the* Winter *book), in ratatouille (page 214), or in a . . . yes! In a cake! This is a bit like carrot cake, but less sweet, I find. Nice!*

FOR THE CAKE
2 cups (150 g) self-rising flour
pinch of salt
2 tsp (1 envelope) vanilla sugar
1 tsp cinnamon
⅔ cup (150 g) packed light brown
　　sugar
1 zucchini, grated
1 cup (150 g) raisins
1 cup (150 g) currants
¾ cup (100 g) hazelnuts, toasted
　　and chopped
2 large eggs
½ cup (125 ml) light olive oil, plus
　　more for greasing

FOR THE LEMON GLAZE
finely grated zest of 1 lemon
1 to 2 tbsp freshly squeezed lemon
　　juice
1½ cups (150 g) confectioners' sugar

Make the cake: Preheat the oven to 350°F (170°C). Grease a 1½-quart (1 l) pan with oil. Line the bottom with parchment paper and grease the paper.

In a large bowl, sift the flour together with the salt, vanilla sugar, and cinnamon. Add the brown sugar, zucchini, raisins, currants, and hazelnuts and toss well.

In a small bowl, beat the eggs with the oil. Pour into the other ingredients while stirring.

Pour the batter into the prepared pan. Bake for 60 to 75 minutes, until a skewer inserted in the center comes out clean.

Let the cake cool for 15 minutes. Carefully slide a knife around the edges, then invert the cake onto a rack to cool completely.

Make the lemon glaze: Combine the lemon zest and a few drops of lemon juice with the confectioners' sugar until you have a mixture with the texture of fluid yogurt. Be careful while adding the lemon juice, as it's easy to add too much.

Pour the glaze over the cooled cake and let it set.

The cake will keep, stored in an airtight container, for up to 1 week.

regarde le ciel...

Paris, France

Home

New York, USA

Ardmore, Ireland

walnut and sugar cookies

FOR ABOUT 15 COOKIES

7 tbsp (100 g) unsalted butter, at
 room temperature
2 tsp (1 envelope) vanilla sugar
2 tbsp confectioners' sugar, plus
 more for rolling
1 cup (125 g) all-purpose flour
pinch of salt
about 15 walnut halves (or
 substitute pecans)

Preheat the oven to 400°F (200°C). Line a baking sheet with parchment paper.

In a medium bowl, beat the butter with the vanilla sugar and confectioners' sugar until creamy. Add the flour and salt and mix until just combined. Using your hands, roll the batter into small balls, the size of a walnut. Place them on the lined baking sheet and gently press a nut into each (this will flatten them a little).

Bake for 10 to 12 minutes, until barely golden. Make sure they don't brown.

Let the cookies cool for about 5 minutes, then roll them—while still hot—in confectioners' sugar to coat. Let them cool completely, then roll them in confectioners' sugar once more.

chocolate chunky cookies

They really don't take much time to make, but be aware that the dough has to firm up in the fridge for a few hours. (Just in case you're dying to eat chewy chocolate cookies right now.)

FOR ABOUT 36 COOKIES

2 cups (250 g) self-rising flour
pinch of salt
½ cup plus 1 tbsp (125 g) unsalted
 butter
2¾ oz (75 g) dark chocolate, cut
 into chunks, plus another 3½ oz
 (100 g) finely chopped
1 cup (200 g) sugar
2 large eggs
1 teaspoon vanilla extract, or 2 tsp
 (1 envelope) vanilla sugar

Combine the flour and salt in a small bowl. In a small saucepan over low heat, melt the butter, then turn off the heat and add the 2¾ oz (75 g) chocolate in chunks. Let the mixture stand for 10 minutes, until all the chocolate has melted, then stir until smooth and pour into a large bowl.

Add the sugar, eggs, and vanilla and whisk swiftly until smooth. While stirring, pour in the flour and the 3½ oz (100 g) finely chopped chocolate. Mix until combined. The dough will be somewhat soft. Cover the dough and place the bowl in the fridge to firm up for a few hours or, better still, overnight.

Preheat the oven to 350°F (175°C). Grease two baking sheets.

Use your hands to shape the dough into small balls the size of walnuts and arrange them, slightly apart, on the baking sheets. Bake for 10 to 12 minutes, until just firm to the touch. Let them cool on a rack.

Châteaurenard, Provence, France

Paris

éclairs with lavender filling

This is Sophie. She has worked in the kitchen of our restaurant for a long time and is French. Whenever I return from Paris she always asks me to bring an éclair for her, since what we Dutch have with *moorkoppen* (a cream puff pastry filled with whipped cream and glazed with dark chocolate) is what the French have with éclairs.

Fortunately, as with so many things, you can make éclairs yourself, and Sophie loves to show me how. Are you tagging along?

1. In a heavy saucepan, **bring** 3½ tbsp (50 ml) water, 3½ tbsp (50 ml) milk, a pinch of salt, 1 tsp superfine sugar, and 3 tbsp (40 g) butter to a boil. Add ½ cup (60 g) all-purpose flour and stir with a wooden spatula until the dough comes away from the sides of the pan. **2**. **remove** from the heat and, bit by bit, stir in 2 beaten eggs. You may not need all the egg, says Sophie; once the mixture resembles the texture of thick béchamel, it's ready. **3**. **spoon** the dough into a pastry bag. (Use a pitcher to support the bag so you won't need an extra hand.) **4**. **pipe** "sausages" 5 to 6 inches (12 to 15 cm) long on baking sheets lined

with parchment paper, using a wet finger to round the tips. Bake the pastries at 350°F (180°C) for 15 minutes, until golden brown. Turn off the oven and leave the pastries in it to cool. **5. combine** 1¼ cups (300 ml) milk with 3 tbsp (35 g) sugar, 1 split vanilla bean, and 1½ tsp lavender flowers in a small saucepan over low heat. Let the mixture steep for 15 minutes over low heat. Strain and discard the lavender. **6. whisk** 3 egg yolks with 3 tbsp (35 g) sugar in a bowl until foamy, add ¼ cup (35 g) cornstarch, and stir until smooth. Stirring constantly, pour in the infused milk. Pour the mixture back into the saucepan and cook over low heat, stirring, until it thickens to the consistency of thick yogurt. **7. stir** in 2 tbsp (30 g) unsalted butter in

chunks. Pour the crème patissière into a pastry bag and let it cool. **8. make** a small hole with a knife at one end of each pastry and pipe pastry cream into each. **9. sift** 1 cup (100 g) confectioners' sugar into a bowl and stir in 1 tbsp water or milk to make a smooth glaze; add food coloring if you wish. The glaze should be thick enough to coat the back of a spoon. If it's too thin, add some confectioners' sugar; if it's too thick, add a drop of water. Do it drop by drop, as sometimes 1 drop can be too much—it sounds silly but it's true, trust me. **10. spread** the tops of the filled pastries with the glaze. **11. let** the éclairs dry on a rack. Serve them immediately or keep in the fridge in an airtight container until ready to serve.

Paris

Barcelona

red iced tea

FOR 4 SERVINGS

1 red grapefruit
1 cup (250 ml) cranberry juice
6 large (100 g) strawberries
2 cups (500 ml) brewed Earl Grey
    tea, chilled
up to 3 tbsp honey if you wish,
    though I don't use it

Juice the grapefruit and pour the juice into a blender with the other ingredients. Blend until smooth. Strain into a glass pitcher with lots of ice cubes.

refreshing summer tea

FOR 6 CUPS (1½ L)

1 bunch of fresh mint leaves (about
    ½ cup/20 g)
1 tbsp dried lemon verbena
    (available in specialty tea stores)
1 stalk lemongrass, bruised and
    twisted into a knot
2 slices fresh ginger
honey for serving

Boil 6 cups of water. In a glass pitcher, combine the mint, lemon verbena, lemongrass, and ginger. Pour boiling water in and let it steep.

Serve with nice honey.

You can serve this tea hot or cold.

mango & cilantro iced tea

FOR 6 CUPS (1½ L)

1 fresh mango, peeled and sliced
1 cup (250 ml) pineapple juice
4 to 6 sprigs fresh cilantro
4 cups (1 l) strong green tea, cooled
1 to 2 tbsp honey

In a blender, puree the mango with the pineapple juice and cilantro leaves until smooth. Pour the cold tea into a large pitcher and stir in the mango-pineapple juice. Stir in honey to taste.

Place in the fridge to chill.

Serve with lots of ice cubes.

(This drink isn't pictured.)

raspberry lemonade

FOR A GENEROUS 6 CUPS (1½ L)

juice of 4 lemons
juice of 4 limes
1¼ cups (250 g) sugar
½ pint (250 g) fresh raspberries
4 cups (1 l) ice-cold water (still or
    sparkling)
lime slices

In a large pitcher, stir the juices with the sugar until the sugar is dissolved.

Puree two thirds of the raspberries in a blender and strain, discarding the seeds. Add the juice to the lemon-lime mixture and stir. Stir in the water.

Divide the rest of the raspberries and the lime slices among a few glasses and pour in the lemonade.

(This drink isn't pictured.)

MINT LEMMO

hot summer days simply beg
for this drink.
Really, I've heard it myself.

→ BRING 1¼ CUPS (50G)
MINT LEAVES WITH
1¼ CUPS (300 ml) WATER,
1 CUP (200 G) SUGAR
& 1 SLICED LEMON
TO A BOIL.
TURN OFF THE HEAT AFTER
5 MINS & LET IT STAND
FOR 1 HOUR. → TO STEEP.

STRAIN THE SYRUP, RETURN
IT TO THE PAN, AND BRING
IT TO A BOIL.
OVER LOW HEAT LET IT
SIMMER FOR ABOUT 15 MINS
UNTIL YOU FIND IT SYRUPY ENOUGH. (WHEN
IT COOLS DOWN, IT WILL BECOME EVEN
MORE SYRUPY!)

MINT

→ POUR THE SYRUP IN AN ULTRACLEAN
BOTTLE. PUT IT IN THE FRIDGE; IT'LL
KEEP FOR MONTHS.

DRINK WITH ICE-COLD SPARKLING
WATER, FRESH MINT &
LEMON SLICES ◄──────

TIP! MAKE THIS SYRUP WITH SAGE INSTEAD
OF MINT.
ANOTHER TIP! ADD A SPLASH OF GIN OR VODKA
FOR A PERFECT APÉRITIF.

berry syrup

1½ pints (500 g) berries, any kind,
    cleaned and halved if necessary
1¾ cups (350 g) sugar

Bring the berries, sugar, and 1 cup (250 ml) water to a boil in a large copper pan. Let simmer for about 15 minutes, until somewhat thickened.

Strain the syrup through a fine sieve into an ultraclean bottle. If you find it too thin, you can pour it back into the pan and boil it down until it thickens. Once cooled, it will thicken some more.

Of course you should keep the fruit pulp and use it on your *Home Made* white wine sorbet (page 233).

tip!

* You can use any fruit in this recipe: make strawberry syrup, peach syrup, apricot syrup, grape syrup.

lemon lemmo

1¾ cups (350 g) sugar
juice of 6 lemons (1¼ cups/300 ml)

In a saucepan over medium-high heat, bring the sugar and lemon juice to a gentle boil and stir until the sugar is dissolved. Pour the syrup in a squeaky-clean bottle and keep it in the fridge.

With sparkling water this will make a delicious drink on a hot day.

tips!

* Replace lemon with orange.

* Add 1 inch grated fresh ginger, let steep, and strain the syrup before you pour it into the bottle.

* Add mint leaves to the glass of lemmo.

* Add a handful of fresh rose petals or dried jasmine (from a specialty tea store) to the syrup in the pan, turn off the heat, and let it steep for about 1 hour, then strain it into the bottle.

clear virgin mary

1½ lb (2 kg) tomatoes, diced
½ cucumber, diced, plus more for
    garnish
1 celery rib, diced
2 tbsp prepared horseradish, or
    1 tbsp very finely grated fresh
      horseradish
sea salt and freshly ground black
    pepper
1 tbsp sugar
lemon slices

In a blender, puree the tomatoes, cucumber, celery, and horse-radish until smooth.

Strain through a sieve lined with cheesecloth into a big bowl. Let the mixture drain, without stirring it, until you have about 3 cups (750 ml) of liquid. This will take about 2 hours, so go ahead and do something else in the meantime.

Season the drink with sea salt, pepper, and the sugar, cover, and store in the fridge until ready to use.

Pour into tall glasses and add ice cubes, lemon slices, and cucumber slices.

You might as well add a splash of vodka. It won't be virgin anymore, but oh, well.

queen's day

on april 30 the dutch
celebrate queen's day, on the
birthday of the late queen
juliana. if you don't happen to
live in the netherlands, imagine a
celebration similar to st. patrick's
day in ireland or the united states,
or bastille day in france.

it comes down to a day of serious
partying—mostly on the eve of
queen's day.

naturally everyone wears something
in the traditional color, orange.

children and parents have stoop
sales and perform tricks or play
instruments for money, and the
diehards continue their partying
throughout the day.

we invariably make our annual
boat tour along the canals of
amsterdam, to check out the
people and the atmosphere. there's
always an awful lot to see.

and we try to sip our drinks
carefully—that is, if after our
debaucheries of the previous night,
we want to.

1. thoroughly rinse 1 orange and 1 lemon with hot water. Dry thoroughly and peel thinly. Make sure to peel off only the colored zest, not the white! **2.** arrange the zest on a baking sheet and dry in a convection oven at 125°F (50°C) max for about 1 hour, or until they are firm and crisp. If you don't have a convection oven, leave the zest to dry in the sun for 5 to 7 days. **3.** in a mortar, combine 1 tbsp anise seeds and 8 cardamom pods and bruise them roughly. **4.** place the bruised seeds in a big jar (at least 1 pint/½ liter) with 3 tbsp lemon juice and the dried citrus zest. Add 2 cups (500 ml) vodka. **5.** seal and let stand for 3 weeks in a warm spot. Shake the jar every other day. **6.** set a sieve lined with a clean dish towel over a big bowl and pour the mixture through. **7.** heat 2 cups (500 ml) water with ⅓ cup (75 g) packed light brown sugar and stir until the sugar is dissolved. Let the syrup cool and add it to the citrus mixture in the bowl. **8.** store the orange bitters in a pretty 1-quart (1-l) bottle. I like it best with some sparkling water, a slice of orange, and lots of ice.

orange bitters

Orange bitters, which we drink on Queen's Day in the Netherlands, is actually really good, but I only found that out when I made it myself. It's pretty different from the obligatory neon-orange shot that I normally down on April 30. I could drink this version all summer long.

coconut summer cocktail

FOR 4 GLASSES

1 fresh coconut
juice of 2 limes
⅓ cup plus 2 tbsp (100 ml) gin
⅓ cup plus 2 tbsp (100 ml) white rum
¾ cup plus 1 tbsp (200 ml) bitter
    lemon
2 to 3 tbsp ginger syrup
3 tbsp dried flaked coconut
    (optional, for garnish)

Hammer a nail into two of the eyes (dark spots) on the coconut to create two small holes. Drain the coconut water through one of the holes into a glass. Wrap the coconut in an old dishcloth, place it on a firm surface outside (on your stoop, for example) and use a hammer to break the coconut. Using a sharp knife, cut the meat out of the coconut. With a vegetable peeler, slice a few pieces of coconut in elegant curves. Set aside.

Reserve 1 tbsp of the lime juice in a small bowl, and put the rest in a blender with 6 ice cubes, the coconut water, gin, rum, bitter lemon, and ginger syrup. Blend into a foamy drink.

Put the flaked coconut in a small bowl alongside the bowl of lime juice. Dip the rims of 4 glasses in the lime juice and then in the coconut. Let them dry. Pour the drink into the prepared glasses and sprinkle with the fresh coconut curls.

PIMM'S CUP

THIS IS WHAT I LIKE TO DRINK!

FOR 1 QUART (1 L):

1 CUP (250 ML) PIMMS № 1 LIQUEUR
1½ CUPS (375 ML) LEMONADE &
1½ CUPS (375 ML) GINGER ALE

½ CUCUMBER CUT INTO THIN ROUNDS

HANDFUL OF FRESH MINT
½ LEMON, CUT INTO THIN SLICES

↓

FILL A PITCHER WITH THIS & A HEAP OF ICE CUBES.

IT'LL BE GONE BEFORE YOU KNOW IT

Cava sangria with Yvette, Amsterdam

cava sangria

2 peaches, sliced
1 orange, thinly sliced
handful of strawberries, raspberries,
    or grapes, halved if large
2 cups (500 ml) freshly squeezed
    grapefruit or orange juice
3 cinnamon sticks
a few sprigs of fresh mint
½ cup (125 ml) brandy (optional)
1 bottle cava (Spanish sparkling wine)

Combine all the fruit and the citrus juice in a big glass pitcher. Add the cinnamon sticks and 2 sprigs of mint, cover, and place in the fridge for 1 hour.

Once your guests have arrived, remove the cinnamon sticks and stir in the brandy (if you wish). Then pop open the cava and pour it on top. Garnish the sangria with some extra fresh mint and top it off with a heap of ice cubes.

Serve the sangria as an apéritif on a warm summer night.

cocktails

This is my hip cousin Alex. He too works in our restaurant and we call him the King of Cocktails. You need to have a feel for making cocktails. Just like when you're cooking, you need a good sense of whether a drink needs more or less sweetness, tartness, bitterness, or alcohol. With Alex this all comes naturally, and he makes drinks from scratch and by taste rather than measurements.

To help you make them exactly like he does, though, I've written it all down.

elder blossom collins

FOR 1 COCKTAIL **1.** **for** 1 glass you'll need: 1 part gin, ½ part Lillet Blonde (or dry vermouth), 1 part elderflower syrup (from an organic grocer or see the recipe in *Home Made*), a lot of ice, sparkling water, and a stick of cucumber. **2.** **combine** the gin, Lillet, and elderflower syrup in a glass filled with ice. **3.** **stir** well with the cucumber stick. **4.** **top** off with sparkling water and serve with the cucumber stick. The taste of the cucumber will seep in and that makes this a wonderfully refreshing drink.

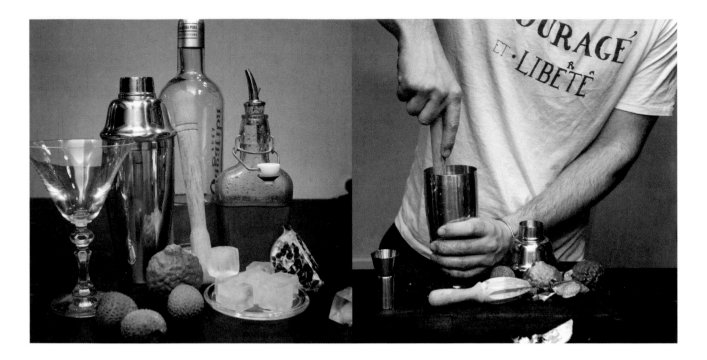

pink and juicy

1. you need: ¼ pomegranate, 2 lychees, 2 parts cachaça, 1 part "Sophie's syrup" (*for that, boil 1 cup [250 ml] water, 1¼ cups [250 g] sugar, grated zest of 1 lemon and ½ orange, and seeds from 1 vanilla bean; strain and let cool, then stir in ⅓ cup [75 ml] rum*), juice of 1 lemon, and a handful of ice cubes. **2. peel** the fruits and muddle them well with the other ingredients (except the ice) in the shaker. **3. add** the ice cubes and shake thoroughly. **4. strain** into a fancy glass. Alex cuts a snazzy lime curl to garnish it.

the alexander

1. you need: 1 part bourbon, ½ part Ramazzotti (or another amaro like Averna), ½ part red vermouth (Alex likes Antica Formula, or Lillet Rouge if he wants it to be a tad sweeter, but you can also use Martini or Cinzano), a tiny dash of Angostura bitters, a handful of ice cubes, and 1 maraschino cherry. **2**. measure the spirits precisely into a glass of ice. **3**. stir the drink with a spoon. **4**. serve with one of those cheerful cherries. It's a knockout drink, but I'm quite fond of it.

negroni fig ice pops

FOR 4 TO 6 ICE POPS

½ cup plus 2 tbsp (150 ml) red
    vermouth
2½ tbsp (40 ml) gin
½ cup (125 ml) freshly squeezed
    orange juice
3 fresh figs
⅓ cup (75 ml) golden syrup or
    clover honey

Put everything in a blender and blend until completely smooth.
Pour through a sieve into a bowl with a spout and then pour
into 4 to 6 ice pop molds.

Place in the freezer and push wooden sticks in after 2 hours.

Freeze for at least another 4 hours, but ideally for 1 day.

Run the ice pops under hot running water for 3 seconds to
unmold them.

TO START

Dublin, Ireland

Paris, France.

Oysters at a Sunday market on Richard Lenoir, Paris

oysters

During the midsummer months of June and July, oysters are hard to come by because that's when they reproduce. But don't worry, you can find them in spring and in late summer, and I think they're one of the most delicious things on earth. That's why, in our restaurant, we have them on the menu throughout the year. In the middle of summer in Paris you'll only find Gillardeau oysters, but those are among my favorites.

Buying a crate directly from a fishmonger is not as expensive as you might think, and opening the oysters yourself really isn't the enormous endeavor most people take it to be.

I'll explain the process to you in clear and simple terms, if you promise to prepare oysters once in a while. Trust me: Your friends will love you even more for it.

You'll need at least 2 or 3 oysters per person (or more, of course).

See what your fishmonger has on offer: Try a couple varieties to discover which ones you like.

opening the oysters

This requires some practice, but no worries: It's really not that difficult.

As with everything, you just need to try it! Once you've got it down, there's nothing to it.

Hold an oyster in your hand, wrapped tightly in a folded dishcloth. The flat half of the shell should be facing up. Stick an oyster knife—or another sharp, short knife—in the hinge, the point were the two halves are attached. Sometimes it takes some effort to find the right spot. Carefully stick your knife inside and gently pry the two shells apart. Slide the blade along the edge of the shells. Twist the knife to open them. Make sure you hold the oyster horizontal or you'll spill the oyster "liquor."

Throw out the flat shell. Cut the oyster loose from the rounded shell and check for any gravel or sand. Get rid of it because it feels terrible in your mouth.

Pour out half of the liquid from the opened shells to make room for your Home Made *dressing or lemon juice.*

Serve the oysters on a large plate or tray filled with crushed ice. If you don't have an ice crusher, put all the ice cubes from your fridge in a clean dish towel, slam it down on the curb, et voilà: *crushed ice.*

Place one or more small bowls with dressings of your choice in the bed of crushed ice and add some lemon wedges. You can garnish the plate using the flat oyster halves or—why not?—maybe get creative with some seaweed! When you buy a crate of oysters it usually comes with some seaweed to keep the shells damp and to keep them from getting damaged. Otherwise ask your fishmonger; he might have some.

A cool trick for a dashing color effect: If you pour boiling water over the seaweed (do this over the sink), it will turn bright green. Serve the oysters with thinly sliced sourdough bread, a black pepper grinder, and butter or horseradish butter (see Home Made Winter*).*

The sauces on the following pages are all perfect oyster companions.

oyster dressings

raspberry dressing

6 tbsp *Home Made* raspberry vinegar (see page 107)
1 small shallot, minced

Combine the vinegar and shallot in a small bowl. Place a teaspoon and a pepper grinder next to the bowl; that way everyone can season their oysters as they please.

ginger–lime dressing

juice of 4 limes, grated zest of 1 lime
2 tbsp finely grated fresh ginger
1 clove garlic, finely minced
1 tbsp honey
1 small shallot, minced
salt and freshly ground black pepper

Combine all the ingredients except the salt
and pepper in a small saucepan and bring to a
boil. Let it boil down slightly, then set it aside
to cool. After your dressing has cooled, add
salt and pepper to taste.

sherry–cherry tomato dressing

5 sweet cherry tomatoes
1 tbsp minced fresh chives
6 tbsp sherry vinegar
freshly ground black pepper

Quarter and seed the tomatoes, then cut them
into tiny cubes. Combine them in a small bowl
with the chives and vinegar and season with
some pepper.

raspberry vinegar

Now that summer is here, there are raspberries in abundance. Collect some pretty bottles and make this recipe. It looks lovely on the table, it makes for a perfect gift, and what's more, it takes zero effort.

Did you ever pour a spoonful of homemade raspberry vinegar over a bowl of vanilla ice cream? You should!

2 CUPS (480 ML)

1½ cups (250 g) raspberries
2 cups (500 ml) white wine vinegar
⅓ cup (60 g) superfine sugar

Put the raspberries in a bowl and pour in the vinegar. Cover and let stand at room temperature for 2 weeks. Once in a while, press the raspberries against the side of the bowl with a spoon to release their juice. Place a sieve over a saucepan and pour the raspberries and vinegar into it. Use a spoon to gently press down on the raspberries to drain the juice from them. Be sure not to press down too hard or the vinegar will be cloudy.

Add the sugar to the vinegar and slowly bring the mixture to near boiling, stirring until the sugar has dissolved. Pour the vinegar into spotlessly clean glass bottles and close them off with a cork or a lid. You can keep your home made vinegar in a cool dark room for over 6 months.

tip!

Combining the vinegar with some nut oil and a drop of honey makes a delicious vinaigrette to drizzle over a goat cheese or chicken salad.

melanzane sott'olio

Once again we can't omit Maria from the book. In my first book, Home Made, *I wrote about her. In Amsterdam she cleans our house like a white tornado and she's a ridiculously good source of recipes. Sometimes we tell each other recipes from the top of our heads as if they were fairy tales, or we go over what we had for dinner the previous evening and what we are planning to cook later that day or that weekend. By the time we're finished, the afternoon is already over and we haven't gotten any cleaning done.*

Here is one of her recipes. We once held a contest to see which of us could prepare this the best. Needless to say, I lost that contest by a landslide, if only because Maria is always right.

FOR A 1-QUART (1-L) JAR

4½ lb (2 kg) eggplant
3 tbsp salt
4 cups (1 l) white wine vinegar

SEASONING (YOU CAN TWEAK THIS
HOWEVER YOU LIKE)
1 or 2 fresh hot red peppers
2 cloves garlic, briefly blanched
a few fresh mint sprigs
enough good olive oil to submerge
everything

Peel the eggplants and cut them into slices about ⅓ inch (8 mm) thick. Put them in a large bowl and sprinkle them with the salt. Toss until the eggplant is covered with a nice layer of salt. Place a sheet of plastic wrap directly onto the eggplant and then invert a plate on top, weighted with something heavy, like a can of beans. You want some pressure on the eggplant. Let stand for 24 hours.

Thoroughly rinse the eggplant slices and squeeze them to release the liquid. Use your hands; don't be prissy.

Rinse the bowl and put the eggplant back in. Now add the vinegar and again let the mixture stand for 24 hours (no need to weight it).

Once again try to wring as much as you can from the soaked eggplant.

Now we get to the good part. Slice the peppers into thin rings and the garlic into thin slices, and coarsely chop the mint. Toss with the eggplant slices and stuff everything into a clean glass jar. Add enough oil to completely fill up the jar. Tap on the jar a few times to let out any air bubbles. Seal it and be patient for 3 to 4 days. You can eat it after 3 to 4 days, but it will keep for over a year.

Serve the Melanzane Sott'olio as an antipasto—*before* the starter—with a glass of chilled red wine and, who knows, some nice mozzarella.

In Italy they keep this for over a year, so be sure to make enough so you won't run out.

tip from maria:

You can also make this with red bell pepper, on its own or together with eggplant. If you do this, add fennel seeds instead of mint.

another tip from maria:

Soak 2 bamboo skewers, bend them without completely breaking them, and place them, crossed, in the jar to make sure the eggplants stay covered in oil and prevent them from surfacing.

crispy chickpeas

For the crispiest results, pat the chickpeas dry before you fry them. I wrap them in a dish towel; tossing them around a little usually does the trick. Serve the chickpeas immediately after frying, or they'll soften.

FOR 6 TO 8 SERVINGS

1 tsp paprika and/or just a pinch of
    cayenne, to taste
2 tsp salt
1 tbsp fresh thyme leaves
2 tsp finely grated lemon zest
6 tbsp extra-virgin olive oil
About 3 cups (500 g) dried
    chickpeas, soaked and cooked,
    or 1 (15-oz/430-g) can, rinsed
    and drained, thoroughly dried

In a large bowl, combine the paprika and cayenne (if using it), salt, thyme, and lemon zest.

Heat the oil in a skillet over medium heat. Add half of the chickpeas and fry them, stirring constantly, for about 15 minutes, until they are golden brown and crisp. Scoop them out of the pan with a skimmer and let them drain on paper towels. Fry the remaining chickpeas.

Spoon all the chickpeas into the bowl and toss with the spices. Serve with a drink. I'd go for some beer.

chanterelle pâté

FOR 6 TO 8 PEOPLE

½ cup plus 6 tbsp (200 g) unsalted
    butter
2 tbsp olive oil
5¼ oz (150 g) sliced fresh
    chanterelle mushrooms (or
    other mushrooms)
salt and freshly ground black pepper
1 clove garlic, pushed through a
    garlic press
⅓ cup (75 ml) Marsala or sherry
juice and grated zest of ½ lemon
1 tbsp tomato paste
a few sprigs of fresh flat-leaf parsley,
    chopped

Melt one third of the butter with the oil in a large sauté pan.
Add the mushrooms and sauté for about 5 minutes. Season
with salt and pepper. Add the garlic, Marsala, lemon juice and
zest, and tomato paste. Cook until the liquid has evaporated.
Let cool completely.

Combine the mushroom mixture with the remaining butter in a
food processor and pulse until you have a fairly smooth pâté. Add
the parsley and taste for salt and pepper. Spoon the pâté into a
nice small bowl and let it firm up in the fridge for at least 4 hours.

Serve with drinks . . . and toast!

bread dips

eggplant caviar

3 eggplants (about 2.2 lbs / 1 kg)
olive oil
½ clove garlic, pushed through a garlic press
a few drops of lemon juice and the grated zest of
    ½ lemon
pinch of paprika
salt and freshly ground black pepper

Preheat the broiler to high. Place the eggplants on a baking sheet and place it under the broiler. Flip the eggplants regularly with tongs until very soft. You can allow the skin to turn black and get a little scorched.

Remove the eggplants from the oven and cut them open lengthwise. Scoop the soft warm pulp into a sieve to drain. Let the pulp cool. Mash with a fork and season with oil, garlic, lemon juice and zest, paprika, salt, and pepper.

yogurt dip with mint

1⅓ cups (300 g) thick plain yogurt
juice and grated zest of 1 lemon
2 cloves garlic, pushed through a garlic press
2 tbsp minced fresh mint, plus more leaves for garnish
1 tsp ground coriander
1 tsp honey
salt and freshly ground black pepper
1 tsp coriander seed, cracked in a mortar

In a bowl, stir together the yogurt, lemon juice
and zest, garlic, and minced mint. Season
with the ground coriander, honey, and salt
and pepper. Beware: Never use a mixer or
blender for this dip, or it'll become as runny as
a milkshake—just stir with a spoon. Cover the
dip and let it sit in the fridge for at least 1 hour,
so that the flavors can meld. Before serving,
sprinkle the dip with some fresh mint leaves
and some coriander seeds from the mortar.

white bean hummus

about 1¼ cups (300 g) cooked white beans (or another
    type) or canned beans, drained and rinsed
about 3½ tbsp (50 ml) olive oil, plus some extra
1 clove garlic, pushed through a garlic press
juice and grated zest of ½ lemon
2 tbsp minced fresh flat-leaf parsley
salt and freshly ground black pepper
pinch of cayenne and/or paprika

Combine all the ingredients except the cayenne in a food processor or blender and pulse
to a smooth puree. Spoon the hummus into a
bowl, drizzle with more oil, and sprinkle with
the cayenne or paprika.

PRESERVING YOUR OWN LEMONS

→→→ → EASY ← ←←←

FOR 2 SQUEAKY-CLEAN CANNING JARS

2 × 1 QUART (1 LITER)

ABOUT 12 LEMONS
PLENTY OF SEA SALT
(BY WHICH I MEAN 3½ LB
OR 1½ KG, OR THEREABOUTS)
1¼ CUPS (300 ML)
FRESHLY SQUEEZED
LEMON JUICE
SOME BOILING WATER

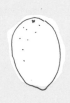

THOROUGHLY RINSE THE LEMONS, THEN PARTIALLY
SPLIT THEM INTO QUARTERS FROM TOP TO BOTTOM
WITH A KNIFE, LEAVING ENOUGH OF THE BOTTOM
INTACT TO HOLD THE QUARTERS TOGETHER.
GENEROUSLY FILL THEM WITH SALT. DIVIDE THE
LEMONS AND LEMON JUICE BETWEEN THE JARS,
THEN SPRINKLE ANOTHER GENEROUS HANDFUL
OF SALT INTO THE JARS, AND FILL WITH BOILING
WATER.
PUT THE LIDS ON TIGHTLY & LET THE JARS SIT
IN A DARK PLACE FOR A GOOD 3 WEEKS.
SHAKE THEM ONCE IN A WHILE.
→ NOW THEY ARE READY TO USE!
RINSE OFF THE LEMON BEFORE YOU USE IT. IN
THE JAR, THESE LEMONS WILL STAY GOOD
FOR AT LEAST A YEAR. ONCE OPENED, KEEP
THE JARS IN THE FRIDGE.

preserved lemons are perfect in stews.
You can also use just the peel, cut
into thin strips, in salads: with
chicken, fish or cheese, for example.
the salty water that's left in the jars
makes for a delicious dressing

salad of quinoa, fava beans, turnip greens & preserved lemon

1⅓ cups (200 g) quinoa, rinsed well

1¾ cups (500 g) shelled fresh fava
    beans (that's 2 ¼ lb [1 kg] in
    the pods)

7 oz (200 g) fresh turnip greens,
    or arugula

1 preserved lemon (page 116), rinsed,
    with the pulp scraped out (don't
    throw it out!)

handful of fresh flat-leaf parsley,
    stemmed

FOR THE PEPPERY DRESSING
preserved lemon pulp from 1 lemon,
    or 2 tbsp freshly squeezed
    lemon juice

1 tbsp honey

⅓ cup (75 ml) light olive oil

½ tsp coriander

freshly ground white pepper

Bring a saucepan of salted water to a boil, add the quinoa, and boil for exactly 10 minutes. Pour the quinoa into a sieve and rinse with cold running water. Bring another saucepan of salted water to a boil and blanch the fava beans for a couple of minutes, until al dente. Drain the beans and rinse them with cold water as well. Large fava beans should be peeled, but if you do not have the patience to do this you can leave them as they are.

Slice the preserved lemon peel into very thin strips.

Make the dressing: Combine all the ingredients in a food processor, giving the white pepper grinder a generous swing. Pulse to combine. Salt isn't really necessary, as the preserved lemon is salty enough.

Just before serving, gently toss together all the ingredients for the salad and drizzle the dressing over it. Serve straight away with some nice roasted meat.

preserved lemon vinaigrette

½ red onion, diced
½ preserved lemon (page 116)
¼ cup (60 ml) olive oil
2 tbsp white wine vinegar
1 tsp honey, or date syrup or brown
    sugar
1 clove garlic, passed through a garlic
    press
1 tsp cumin
1 tsp paprika
1 small bunch of fresh mint,
    chopped
salt and freshly ground black pepper
3 to 4 tbsp plain yogurt

Combine all the ingredients except the yogurt in a blender, season with salt and pepper, and blend to a smooth paste. Stir in the yogurt by hand; the dressing will get very runny if you add the yogurt to the blender.

I love this dressing; it's delicious.

On a spinach salad, with green beans or chickpeas, croutons, and fresh green herbs.

On grilled chicken (page 163) with a Belgian endive salad with nuts and thinly shaved fennel.

On a grain salad made with cooked barley, pearl barley, spelt, or bulgur. Mix with a lot of fresh herbs, dried tomatoes (page 36), pine nuts, and julienned raw zucchini.

On a salad of cooked beluga lentils with strips of blanched (for 10 minutes) Tuscan kale and fresh cilantro.

maria's fritters

Maria, our Italian housekeeper, usually comes to our house after noon. If the weather is nice she'll eat her lunch first, outside; otherwise she'll bring her lunch in and we'll eat together in the kitchen. One day she took a sandwich on dark Dutch bread from her bag and gave me half:

"Taste!" she said.

It was funny, I was tasting Dutch and Italian at the same time: Wow, so good!

"Pumpkin fritters!" she exclaimed proudly, "and I made them from scratch. They're great on some bread, but also just on their own, as an antipasto."

In September or October you'll be able to find pumpkins everywhere—just be sure to use "sweet" or "pie" pumpkins, not the kind you use for jack-o'-lanterns, which are too big and stringy.

9-oz (250-g) piece of pumpkin
1 tsp active dry yeast
4 tbsp all-purpose flour
1 large egg
2 tbsp chopped fresh parsley
salt and freshly ground black pepper
oil for frying
grated zest of ½ lemon

Peel the pumpkin and remove the seeds. Chop the flesh, and boil it in salted water for 8 to 10 minutes, until al dente. Drain well. Meanwhile, combine the yeast with 3 tablespoons lukewarm water in a small bowl.

In a medium bowl, mash the pumpkin and add 3 tbsp of the flour, egg, parsley, and the yeast. Season with salt and pepper and mix well. Cover the bowl and let it stand for 1 hour.

Stir in the reserved tablespoon of flour.

In a deep, heavy pan, heat at least 2 inches of oil over medium-high heat until hot but not smoking. With two spoons, form small balls of the batter and fry them for a few minutes until golden brown, turning them over to brown them on both sides. Drain on paper towels.

Serve immediately, sprinkled with the lemon zest. You can eat any leftovers on a sandwich the next day.

cold green soup with horseradish & garlic hangop

You can also eat this soup warm, but it has a stronger taste when cold, and it's especially great on a hot summer day. Hangop *means, literally, "hang up," which is what you do with this yogurt.*

FOR THE HANGOP

2 cups (500 ml) thick plain yogurt
1 clove garlic, passed through a garlic
    press
pinch of salt
½ bunch garden cress

FOR THE SOUP

4 cups (1 l) chicken or vegetable
    stock
1 cup (250 g) shelled English peas
    (preferably fresh, but frozen
    is fine)
1 cup (250 g) marrowfat peas
    (preferably fresh, but frozen is
    fine; if you can't find marrowfat
    peas, just use more regular
    peas)
6 oz (150 g) fresh spinach, stemmed
⅓ cup (15 g) fresh mint leaves
⅓ cup (75 ml) dry vermouth
1 tbsp freshly grated horseradish, or
    2 tbsp prepared horseradish
salt and freshly ground black pepper

Make the *hangop*: Place a sieve over a large bowl and line the sieve with a clean dish towel. Pour in the yogurt. Stir in the garlic and salt.

Cover the yogurt with some plastic wrap or aluminum foil and put the bowl and sieve in the fridge for 24 hours.

Scrape the *hangop* from the cloth into a bowl and stir in half of the watercress.

Make the soup: In a stockpot, bring the stock to a boil with the English peas and marrowfat peas. Simmer for about 15 minutes, then scoop some of the peas out and reserve them to use as a garnish.

Add the spinach and mint to the pot. Let it simmer for a few minutes; it will wilt right away.

Puree the soup in batches in a blender for about 6 minutes. Puree longer than you would think, as only then will the soup become really smooth. It can be done with an immersion blender instead, but the pea skins can be stubborn. Stir in the vermouth and horseradish, then taste for salt and pepper.

Refrigerate until completely cool.

Ladle the soup into 4 soup bowls. With an ice cream scoop, spoon a small ball of *hangop* into the middle of each bowl and garnish with the remaining watercress and the reserved peas.

cantaloupe soup with goat cheese and basil oil

1 cantaloupe, chilled, seeded and
    peeled
½ cup plus 2 tbsp (150 ml) dry white
    wine
a 1-inch (2-cm) piece of fresh ginger
finely grated zest and juice of
    ½ lemon
freshly ground black pepper
a generous handful fresh basil leaves,
    plus a few extra for garnish
pinch of salt
⅓ cup plus 2 tbsp (100 ml) olive oil
4 oz (125 g) soft goat cheese

In a food processor, puree the melon until smooth.

Add the wine, ginger, lemon zest, and a good grind of black pepper. Puree all into a foamy, smooth soup.

In a mortar, grind the handful of basil with the salt and the lemon juice until smooth. Gently drizzle in the oil and stir until you have a nice green oil.

Ladle the soup into 4 soup bowls and sprinkle each with crumbled fresh goat cheese, a few drops of the basil oil, and the reserved fresh basil leaves.

watercress soup with parmesan flan

FOR 6

FOR THE FLANS

¾ cup plus 1 tbsp (200 ml) heavy
    cream
½ cup (125 ml) whole milk
¾ cup (75 g) grated Parmesan
    cheese, plus some shaved
    Parmesan for garnish
1 large egg
2 large egg yolks
salt and white pepper

FOR THE SOUP

3 spring onions or large scallions,
    finely chopped
2 tbsp olive oil
2 (3-inch / 7.5-cm) potatoes, peeled
    and diced
1 cup (250 ml) dry vermouth
3 cups (750 ml) (*Home Made*)
    vegetable stock
2 bunches watercress, washed and
    stemmed
⅓ cup (75 ml) heavy cream, if you
    wish
salt and freshly ground black pepper

Make the flans: Generously butter 6 small ramekins (¼ cup / 60 ml size).

In a small, heavy saucepan, bring the cream and milk to a gentle boil over medium heat. Add the grated cheese and stir until it's melted. Remove the pan from the heat, cover, and let stand for 30 minutes.

Preheat the oven to 300°F (150°C).

Strain the cream mixture through a fine sieve into a bowl; with the back of a spoon, push all the liquid out.

In a medium bowl, whisk the egg with the egg yolks, and season with salt and white pepper. Pour the cream mixture into the egg mixture in a thin trickle, stirring constantly. Divide the mixture among the ramekins.

Place the ramekins in a large baking dish and add enough water to the dish to come three quarters of the way up the sides of the ramekins. Place the baking dish on a rack in the center of the oven and bake for about 45 minutes, until the flans are just barely set in the center.

Remove the ramekins from the water and let them cool on a rack for at least 5 minutes.

Make the soup: In a large saucepan over medium heat, sauté the onions in the oil until soft. Add the potatoes. Sauté them briefly, douse them with the vermouth, allow it evaporate for a moment, then pour in the stock. Bring to a boil, then lower the heat and simmer until the potatoes are tender, about 15 minutes. Add the watercress. Let everything simmer for 5 to 7 minutes, until the watercress is just tender, then puree the soup with an immersion blender. You can add cream after pureeing for a creamier soup, or you can leave it as is.

Taste for salt and pepper.

Carefully run a sharp knife around the edges of the flans to loosen them from the ramekins. Cover a flan with a soup bowl and invert the flan into the bowl. Carefully lift off the ramekin. Repeat for all the flans.

Surround the flans with a generous ladleful of the soup.

Garnish with some Parmesan curls and black pepper. Serve immediately.

white gazpacho

This is an exceptionally fun recipe that makes me very happy. Why don't you try it? You may well become addicted; that's what happened to me.

Take note: All quantities are approximate. For a punchier soup, add a bit more vinegar; if you prefer a gentler taste, add some more olive oil. Such fun!

Keep the soup in the fridge until ready to serve, or take it along to a picnic in a Thermos.

about ⅓ cup (100 ml) vegetable stock
1 thick slice of white bread, crusts removed
1 clove garlic, passed through a garlic press
½ bunch seedless green grapes (about 25 grapes)
1 cucumber, peeled, seeded, and diced
½ cup (50 g) almonds, preferably smoked
½ cup (125 ml) heavy cream
½ cup (120 g) plain yogurt
2 to 3 tbsp white wine vinegar
3½ tbsp (50 ml) extra-virgin olive oil
salt and freshly ground black pepper
1 avocado, peeled, pitted, and sliced
alfalfa sprouts

Put the stock in a bowl and soak the bread in it for about 5 minutes.

Put the soaked bread in a blender or food processor. Add the garlic, grapes, cucumber, and almonds. Process until smooth; this will take a while, so take your time.

Transfer to a bowl and whisk in the cream, yogurt, vinegar, and oil. Season the soup with salt and pepper only after all ingredients have been thoroughly incorporated.

Put in the fridge—say, for an hour—to chill well.

Serve in shallow bowls, garnished with avocado slices and alfalfa sprouts.

cucumber & papaya soup with lobster

FOR ABOUT 8 SERVINGS

2 (1¾-lb/800-g) live lobsters
juice of ½ large lemon

FOR THE SOUP
2 lb (1 kg) papaya, peeled, seeded,
    and diced
1 cucumber, peeled and diced
2 cups (500 ml) cold chicken broth
½ cup plus 2 tbsp (150 ml) milk
juice of ½ large lemon
splash of good dry sherry
    (manzanilla!)
a few drops of Tabasco sauce
pinch of salt and freshly ground
    black pepper
a few sprigs of fresh tarragon, plus
    more for garnish

After you buy the lobsters, put them in the fridge under a towel, so they'll become a bit drowsy. Add the lemon juice to a large pot of water and bring it to a boil. Boil the lobsters one at a time (putting each in head first, and putting the lid on the pot!) for 8 to 10 minutes, until they are dark red. Take each lobster out of the pot with a skimmer and let it cool on a cutting board.

Halve the lobsters lengthwise with a sharp knife. Remove the meat from the tail and the claws. Use pliers or a hammer! Chill the meat in the fridge.

Make the soup: Puree all the ingredients in a food processor or blender, taste to see if it needs further seasoning, then chill the soup in the fridge until ready to serve.

To serve, ladle the cold soup into 8 soup bowls. Divide the lobster meat among the bowls and garnish with some tarragon leaves and freshly ground pepper.

infused oils

Making herb-infused oils is terribly fun, and they look great on the dinner table. Beware, though: Even a drop of water or other liquid in the oil can cause food poisoning, so if your oils contain water, make sure to keep them in the fridge and discard any unused portion after a week.

This rule applies to water-containing aromatics like garlic, lemon zest, fresh peppers, and fresh herbs. Oils made with dried herbs and spices can be preserved much longer. I never really make much at once, though. After a while (say, six months or so) the oil can become

cinnamon & saffron oil

4 cinnamon sticks
pinch of saffron threads
1 cup (250 ml) light olive oil

In a small saucepan over low heat, warm the cinnamon sticks and saffron in the oil. Let steep over low heat for 15 minutes. Let the oil cool, strain it, and then pour it into a very clean, dry bottle. You could add another 2 cinnamon sticks to the bottle, as it looks so pretty and it allows the oil to steep some more.

coriander & cardamom oil

2 tbsp coriander seeds
10 green cardamom pods
1 cup (250 ml) light olive oil

In a small saucepan over low heat, warm the coriander and cardamom in the oil. Let steep over low heat for 15 minutes. Let the oil cool, then pour it through a sieve into a bowl, then into a very clean, dry bottle. You can add some coriander seeds and cardamom pods to the bottle, as it looks so pretty and it allows the oil to steep some more.

basil oil

1 cup (50 g) fresh basil leaves
1 cup (250 ml) light olive oil
salt and freshly ground black pepper

Blanch the basil leaves for 10 seconds in a saucepan of boiling water. Drain the leaves in a sieve and rinse them under cold water. Dab them dry with a paper towel.

Puree the leaves in a blender or grind them in a mortar until smooth, adding the oil in a thin trickle as you blend. Season the green oil with salt and pepper. Store in the refrigerator for up to 4 days, but bring it to room temperature before use.

bitter. I don't usually use extra-virgin olive oil, as I find it too bitter and too strong. The flavor of the ingredients you add will be strong enough. Use a lighter oil and keep that fancy extra-virgin for other uses.

Use your homemade infused oil as a dip for baguette, drizzle it over salads, pasta, or tabbouleh, rub the oil into chicken or fish before you roast or fry it (or even after cooking), or drip some oil into a bowl of soup.

It looks beautiful, but most of all it's delicious!

lavender oil

I hear you thinking: What would I use this for? Well, it's delicious over sautéed chicken, or a salad with goat cheese and possibly some edible flowers, or maybe with the green soup on page 123.

1½ tsp dried lavender
1 cup (250 ml) light olive oil

In a small saucepan over low heat, warm the lavender in the oil. Let it steep over low heat for 15 minutes. Let it cool, then pour it into a very clean, dry bottle.

provençal oil

2 or 3 sprigs fresh thyme
2 or 3 sprigs fresh rosemary
2 dried hot red peppers
4 dried bay leaves
a few black peppercorns
1 cup (250 ml) light olive oil

Preheat the oven to 125°F (50°C) max. Put the thyme and rosemary on a baking sheet and bake until they are bone-dry, about 1 hour.

Put the herbs, peppers, bay leaves, and peppercorns in a jar, pour the oil on top, and let the mixture stand for at least 2 weeks before using.

lemon verbena oil

3 tbsp dried lemon verbena
1 cup (250 ml) olive oil

Process the lemon verbena briefly in a food processor or mortar to break it up. Add the oil and stir well.

Pour the oil into a small saucepan and bring it to a boil. Remove from the heat and pour through a sieve into a measuring cup with a spout.

Don't stir or press the oil in the sieve or the oil will become cloudy — exercise some patience until it seeps through. Keep the oil in a very clean, dry bottle.

thousand–tomato salad with "home made" goat's milk ricotta and coriander & basil oil

FOR THE RICOTTA (MAKES ABOUT 9 OZ / 250 GRAMS)

6 cups (1½ l) goat's milk

juice of 1 lemon

1 tbsp coriander seeds, lightly toasted in a dry skillet

1 tsp salt

FOR THE SALAD

1¾ lb (750 g) tomatoes, as many different kinds as possible

a few spoonfuls of basil oil (page 132)

juice of 1 lemon

salt and freshly ground black pepper

In a large saucepan over medium-high heat, warm the goat's milk with the lemon juice, coriander, and salt until the milk curdles. Let the mixture boil gently for 3 minutes, or until the whey (the clear part) is clearly separated from the curd (the white part).

Line a sieve with clean cheesecloth, place it over a bowl, and pour the mixture through. You can use the whey to bake soda bread (see my *Winter* book). Wring out the curd in the cheese-cloth as much as possible and place the cloth with the ricotta in a mold with small holes. (This is called a *faiselle* in French, but you can also use a can or cup with some holes poked in the bottom, or you can use the ricotta as it is; you don't even have to mold it.) Place the mold in the sink to drain. The longer you let the cheese drain, the firmer it becomes, so for ricotta it doesn't need to drain for very long (try about 30 minutes). Transfer the cheese to the fridge and let it cool completely.

Make the salad: Slice the tomatoes and arrange them on a large plate. Crumble the ricotta on top and drizzle with some basil oil and lemon juice. Season with salt and pepper and serve immediately.

stuffed, marinated zucchini blossoms with lavender salt

Definitely don't wash the flowers, which would bruise them. Wipe them off and check them for ants or other tiny critters. You don't need to take the pistil out.

⅔ cup (150 g) fresh ricotta
    (page 134)
3 tbsp very finely grated Pecorino
    cheese
8 fresh basil leaves, sliced
lavender salt (see page 25) and
    freshly ground black pepper
8 zucchini blossoms

FOR THE DRESSING
juice of ½ lemon
2 tbsp tarragon vinegar
⅓ cup (75 ml) light oil, such as
    sunflower or grapeseed oil
⅓ cup (75 ml) extra-virgin olive oil
salt and freshly ground black pepper

In a small bowl, mix the ricotta with the Pecorino, basil, and some lavender salt and pepper.

Fill each blossom with a spoonful of the mixture and gently twist the tip to close. Filling the flowers is easiest with a pastry bag, but a small spoon works as well.

Make the dressing: In a small bowl, combine the lemon juice and vinegar, then add the oils in a thin trickle, whisking constantly. Season with salt and pepper.

Pour the dressing into a shallow bowl, place the zucchini flowers in the bowl, and let them marinate for at least 3 hours, flipping them over occasionally. Eat with crusty bread.

artichokes "en cocotte"

This starter became a big hit in our restaurant last summer. It's an idea from Sophie, who has been cooking with us for years. We found it so simple and so delicious that we wanted to give you her recipe.

4 artichokes, stems cut off

FOR THE BÉCHAMEL
1 tbsp unsalted butter
1½ tbsp all-purpose flour
¾ cup plus 1 tbsp (200 ml) milk or
    heavy cream, or a mixture
freshly grated nutmeg
salt and freshly ground black pepper

AND FURTHER
4 fresh small eggs
salt and freshly ground black pepper
8 tbsp grated Gruyère

Bring a large stockpot of salted water to a boil. Add the artichokes and boil for 45 minutes. Drain the artichokes and rinse them under cold water. Let them drain upside down in a colander.

With a sharp knife, remove the inner leaves and the hairy chokes. If you like, you can trip the pointy tops of the artichoke leaves with some scissors. It's a little more work, but makes it so much easier to eat the dish later on!

Make the béchamel: Melt the butter in a heavy saucepan. Add the flour and stir for a few minutes until you have a paste, or roux. Little by little, pour in the milk and stir until the milk is absorbed by the roux and you have a smooth, cohesive sauce. Let the sauce simmer over low heat for about 15 minutes, until the flour's raw flavor has disappeared.

Remove from the heat and season with nutmeg, salt, and pepper.

You can do all this in advance. Keep the artichokes and the béchamel sauce covered in the fridge until ready to use.

Preheat the oven to 350°F (180°C) and place a baking pan of water at the bottom of the oven.

Fill the cavity of the scooped-out artichokes with 2 generous tbsp of the béchamel. Carefully crack an egg into the cavity, making sure the yolk remains intact. Season with salt and grind some pepper on top; sprinkle with the Gruyère. Place the artichokes on a baking sheet and bake for 15 minutes, until the egg white has set and the yolk is still soft.

Serve immediately. You can dip the leaves in the sauce in the middle, and the heart . . . oh!

You can turn this into a real meal if you serve it with potatoes *sauce gribiche* (page 217).

Georges, Provence, France

Wim Bijma's vegetable garden, Amsterdam

smoked trout (or mackerel) salad

SERVES 2 OR 3 AS A LUNCH DISH,
OR 4 AS A STARTER

FOR THE DRESSING
3 tbsp buttermilk
2 tbsp mayonnaise
½ tbsp finely grated fresh
    horseradish, or 1 tbsp prepared
    horseradish
2 to 3 tbsp minced fresh chives
2 tbsp extra-virgin olive oil
salt and freshly ground black pepper

FOR THE SALAD
3½ oz (100 g) arugula
2 heads little gem lettuce, or 2 small
    heads romaine, very finely
    chopped
1 Granny Smith apple
juice of ½ lemon
2 smoked trout fillets, or 1 smoked
    mackerel fillet
toast for serving

Make the dressing: In a small bowl, whisk the buttermilk, mayonnaise, horseradish, and chives thoroughly, then trickle in the oil, whisking constantly. Season with salt and pepper.

Make the salad: Toss the arugula with the lettuce. Julienne the apple (leave the skin on), and sprinkle it with the lemon juice. Pull the fish from the bones and toss the fish and the apple with the lettuce mixture. Spoon the dressing on top, toss, and serve the immediately in nice coupes, with toast.

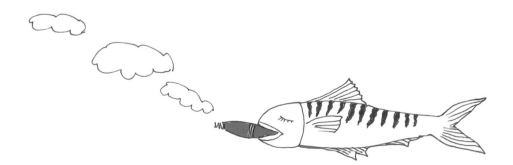

asparagus risotto with samphire

1 bunch asparagus (about 16 stalks)
2 shallots, diced
1 or 2 hot green chiles, sliced,
    seeds removed
1⅔ cups (300 g) risotto rice
    (Vialone Nano or Arborio)
3 tbsp (50 g) unsalted butter
½ cup (150 ml) white wine
small pinch of saffron threads
about 4 cups (1 l) hot vegetable
    stock
5 oz (150 g) samphire (sea beans),
    washed
salt and freshly ground black pepper
Parmesan for grating

Bring a large saucepan of water to a boil. Trim the ends of the asparagus and blanch the stalks for about 2 minutes. Drain and rinse under cold water. Halve the stalks on the diagonal, then halve them lengthwise. Set aside.

In a large saucepan, sauté the shallots, chiles, and rice in half the butter. Stir continuously for 3 minutes, until the rice is shiny and the grains are translucent. Douse the rice with the wine, and keep stirring.

Add the saffron and continue to stir.

Add a ladleful of hot stock to the rice and stir until the stock is absorbed. Keep adding ladlefuls of stock as it is absorbed, and just keep stirring. After 20 minutes the rice should be al dente and the liquid thick and creamy. You may need more or less stock to achieve this consistency. If needed, you can add some salt at the end.

In a separate skillet, sauté the samphire in the remaining butter for 4 to 5 minutes, until it is just tender. Stir the samphire and butter into the risotto. Season the dish with salt and pepper.

Remove the risotto from the heat, cover it, and let it sit for 5 minutes to set. Spoon the risotto onto plates and arrange the asparagus on top. Sprinkle with some Parmesan and serve immediately.

Tomatoes in Wim Bijma's greenhouse, Amsterdam

The Camargue, France

scallop ceviche

SERVES 3 FOR LUNCH OR 4 AS
A STARTER

1 lb (500 g) scallops, cleaned
8 limes
2 medium tomatoes, or 6 to 8
    cherry tomatoes
3 scallions
2 ribs celery
handful of fresh cilantro leaves
salt and freshly ground black pepper
a few drops of good-quality olive oil

Cut the scallops horizontally into 3 or 4 thin slices and arrange them on a large plate.

Juice the limes and pour the juice over the scallop slices. Cover the scallops and place the plate in the fridge for 2 to 3 hours, until the scallops are opaque white.

Pour off about half of the lime juice.

Dice the tomatoes, or, if using cherry tomatoes, cut them into quarters. Thinly slice the scallions and celery. Finely chop the cilantro.

Spoon the vegetables and cilantro onto the marinated scallops. Season with salt, grind some fresh black pepper over them, and drizzle some oil on top.

Eat with crusty bread.

rillettes

Rillettes: *a rustic version of pâté. "Rustic version" meaning zero effort, easy, and most important, almost no ingredients. You can easily do it yourself. I use pork cheeks, wonderfully tender meat, but you can also use pork belly. You can really use any kind of meat as long as you stew it for long enough and the meat isn't too fancy. Why don't you try it with rabbit, goose, duck, or other poultry? This is a basic recipe; you can season it any way you want. Use pork fat, as here, or goose fat. Your butcher will have both, I hope.*

1. **cube** 4½ lb (2 kg) pork cheek. 2. **melt** a nice chunk of pork or goose fat and then sear the meat with a few sprigs of thyme, some bay leaves, generous black pepper, and salt in a heavy cast-iron skillet over medium-high heat. Cover the pan, reduce the heat to low, and let stew for about 3 hours, stirring occasionally. 3. **remove** the thyme, bay leaves, and any bones and finely mince the meat in a food processor. Season well with salt and lots of pepper. 4. **fill** small, squeaky-clean jars with the rillettes. In a small saucepan, melt sufficient pork fat (at least ⅔ cup/150 g) and pour it over the rillettes in the jars to cover the meat completely. Close the jars tightly and let the fat solidify. Store the rillettes in the refrigerator, where they'll keep for a while if you take care to cover the meat with fat whenever you scoop any out, and always use a clean, dry spoon so no water gets into the rillettes.

bacalao & shrimp potpies

I'm writing this recipe for my friend Mo, who, after she'd eaten this in our restaurant, wrote to me that she had to have this recipe because she'd dreamed of the meal. Maybe the same thing will happen to you, so I'm giving it to you, too—with lots of thanks to Jessica, who dutifully wrote this down with me.

Be sure to start this recipe a day in advance, as the salt cod will need to soak for at least 24 hours.

FOR 4 TO 6 POTPIES

10½ oz (300 g) bacalao (salt cod)
10½ oz (300 g) large shrimp, peeled and deveined, or a mix of smaller and larger ones
2 cups (500 ml) fish stock (there's a recipe in *Home Made* to make it yourself)
1 cup (250 ml) heavy cream
1 cup (250 ml) crème fraîche
⅓ cup plus 2 tbsp (100 ml) white wine
dash of Pernod
a few sprigs of fresh tarragon, dill, and/or flat-leaf parsley, minced
grated zest of 1 lemon
pinch of freshly grated nutmeg
pinch of cayenne
pinch of curry powder
pinch of sugar
4 tbsp (60 g) unsalted butter
1 sheet frozen puff pastry, thawed
1 large egg, beaten

TOGETHER UNDER ONE ROOF!

YESSS SIR

Soak the bacalao in a large bowl of cold water for 24 hours, draining the salty water and replacing it with fresh at least 3 times.

In a large saucepan of fresh water, poach the pieces of fish at a simmer for at least 35 minutes. Remove the fish with a skimmer and add the shrimp to the simmering water in the same pan for 1 to 2 minutes, just until they turn opaque and start to curl.

Remove the fish bones, and the skin if you wish, and finely chop the fish.

In a medium saucepan over medium-high heat, combine the stock, cream, crème fraîche, and wine, and bring just to a boil. Reduce the heat to low and boil gently until the sauce is reduced to about 1½ cups (350 ml); this will take about 1 hour, so you can go do something else. Make a salad as a side dish, for example. (See below for a suggestion.)

Season the sauce with Pernod, the herbs, lemon zest, nutmeg, cayenne, curry powder, and sugar. Stir in the butter at the end and remove the pan from the heat. Stir in the fish and shrimp.

Preheat the oven to 350°F (180°C).

Fill single-serving ovenproof dishes with the fish mixture and cut out little lids the size of the dishes from the puff pastry; cut a hole in the center of each with an apple corer or a knife (to allow steam to escape so the pastry can become crisp), then place the lids on top of the bowls and press down the edges. Garnish the lids with leftover pieces of dough. You can make the potpies in advance to this point and refrigerate them, covered with plastic wrap, for up to 2 days.

Brush the puff pastry with the beaten egg. Bake the potpies for 10 to 12 minutes, until golden and bubbling. If you've made the pies in advance and refrigerated them, they'll need about 25 minutes of baking time.

At Aan de Amstel, our restaurant, we serve them with a small salad of cabbage, mesclun, carrot, julienned apple, and chervil, with a dressing of horseradish, mustard, honey, and white wine vinegar, mixed with some grapeseed oil. Sprinkle with cumin seeds.

Paris

Barcelona

Paris

153

154

Our kitchen in Provence

Our kitchen in Paris

Schellingwoude

MAIN COURSES

pork rib roast with warm, buttery gremolata and roasted garlic

A meat thermometer will come in handy here. It's not absolutely necessary, but if you happen to see one, buy it. They're only a few bucks and they'll save you a lot of guesswork.

FOR AT LEAST 6 PEOPLE, OR IN
OUR CASE 4 (IT'S JUST SO GOOD)

4½-lb (2-kg) pork rib roast (ask
    your butcher to remove the
    vertebrae and the skin but leave
    the fat)
a large bunch of parsley
    (2½ oz/60 g)
⅓ cup plus 2 tbsp (100 ml) extra-dry
    vermouth
3 tbsp (50 g) unsalted butter, at
    room temperature
3½ tbsp (50 ml) olive oil
1 tbsp salt
1½ tsp red pepper flakes or ground
    black pepper
2 heads garlic

Preheat the oven to 350°F (175°C).

Score the layer of fat on the outside of the roast with a sharp knife. I like to make a checkered pattern, but you can also just carve a few parallel straight lines, I leave that up to you. Place the roast in the middle of a roasting pan.

In a food processor, combine all the remaining ingredients except the garlic and pulse to a thick sauce. The butter will remain visible in small bits, but those will melt in the oven.

Reserve a little of the sauce for later, and rub the remaining sauce over the entire roast. Place the garlic heads in the roasting pan. Roast for 1½ hours. If you use a meat thermometer, the core temperature you're looking for is 150°F (65°C). This will leave the center nicely rose colored.

Remove the roast from the oven, remove the heads of garlic from the pan, and cover the roast with aluminum foil. Let the roast rest for 15 minutes.

Meanwhile, warm the reserved sauce in a small saucepan over low heat. Pour the juices from the roasting pan into a container and skim off the clear fat with a spoon and discard it. Pour the juices into the warmed sauce. Squeeze the mushy roasted garlic cloves into a bowl. Carve the rib roast at the table and serve it with the sauce and the garlic in separate bowls.

lamb roast stuffed with oregano, mint, garlic & pine nuts

1 head of garlic, separated into
    cloves
3 handfuls of mixed fresh oregano,
    parsley, and mint
1¾ oz (50 g) anchovy fillets
1 cup (100 g) bread crumbs
grated zest of 1 lemon
1 cup (100 g) pine nuts
½ cup (75 g) golden raisins
3 to 4 tbsp olive oil
salt and freshly ground black
    pepper
1 (3½- to 4½-lb; 1½- to 2-kg) leg of
    lamb of good pedigree, boned

Peel the garlic cloves and put them in a food processor with the herbs, anchovies, bread crumbs, and lemon zest. Grind coarsely. Transfer the mixture to a bowl and add the pine nuts, raisins, and a couple of tablespoons of the oil. Stir your crunchy stuffing mixture and grind some pepper over it. Be sparse with salt, as the anchovies are pretty salty!

Place the lamb flat on the counter in front of you, meat side up. Spread the stuffing over the meat and roll it up. Tie your lamb with butcher's twine, creating a nice tight roll. Rub the roast with salt and pepper and refrigerate for at least 1 hour, but preferably longer, so the flavors meld. In our restaurant we like to refrigerate it overnight. Take the meat out of the fridge 1 hour before you start roasting.

Preheat the oven to 350°F (180°C). Roast the lamb for 1 hour to 1 hour 15 minutes, depending on its weight: 15 minutes per pound (500 g) plus an extra 15 minutes is a good starting point. If you like your meat well done you'll have to roast it a little longer. Turn the roast over halfway through the cooking and occasionally baste it with its own juices.

Place the meat on a cutting board, cover it with aluminum foil, and let it rest for 15 minutes before slicing it.

tip!

After 30 minutes, add some small potatoes to the roasting pan. That way the potatoes can sizzle along with the lamb and everything will be ready at the same time. Parboil larger potatoes for 10 minutes before adding them.

beer can chicken

Yes, you're reading this correctly. Perhaps you regularly fire up the backyard grill and you've heard of this dish before, but for those of you who have no idea what I'm talking about: You stuff an opened can of beer inside a chicken, which lets you roast the chicken sitting upright, and the evaporating beer also makes your roasted chicken extra juicy while enhancing its flavor from the inside out. Isn't that amazing?

Roasting an entire chicken on a barbecue grill is quite a hassle, but using this method you'll be able to pull it off. For a truly juicy result, I brine the chicken the night before. In our restaurant we also do this with poussins and coquelets, or turkey. It's the best way to prepare a juicy bird.

Even if you don't plan to light up the backyard grill, don't flip this page: Just roast the chicken in your oven, sitting on a can of ale or simply lying in a roasting pan.

It's up to you. As a variation, you can also try the rubs on page 164.

FOR THE BRINE
1⅔ cups (500 g) salt
2½ cups (500 g) sugar
2 tbsp juniper berries, bruised in a
     mortar
3 bay leaves, crumbed
1 tbsp black peppercorns
1 tbsp coriander seed

FOR THE CHICKEN
1 whole organic chicken
a few cloves garlic, peeled
a few sprigs fresh thyme and/or
     rosemary
grated zest of 1 lemon
salt and freshly ground black pepper
1 can brown ale, or stout

Make the brine: In a large saucepan, combine all the ingredients with 4 to 6 cups (1 to 1½ l) water and bring to a boil. Stir until the salt and sugar are dissolved. Pour the brine into a container or pot that's large enough to contain the whole chicken but still fits in your fridge, and let it cool completely. When the brine is cool, add the bird and make sure it's submerged. Cover and set aside in the fridge for 24 hours.

Preheat the oven to 350°F (175°C) or prepare a fire in a charcoal grill.

Remove the chicken from the brine and pat it dry with paper towels. Chop the garlic, thyme, and/or rosemary and combine them in a small bowl with the lemon zest and a little salt and pepper. Reserve about 1 tbsp of the rub and spread the remainder over the entire chicken. The chicken is already flavorful, so there's not much you have to add, but this does make for a nice, crisp skin later on. Alternatively, you can season the chicken with your own favorite mix of spices or one of the rubs on page 164.

Open the entire top of the beer can with a can opener, for a nice large hole. Take a few sips—careful!—until about two thirds of the beer is left. Stir the reserved rub into the beer and then shove the can, opening up, into the chicken cavity. See if the chicken will sit upright on the countertop and adjust if necessary; it's much harder to do this later on the hot grill. I always stuff some lemon wedges and thyme into the cavities under the bird's wings.

Stand the chicken in a roasting pan and slide it into the oven or place the chicken directly on the grill once the charcoals are glowing red and have formed a thin layer of ash. Cover the grill. After 1 hour to 1 hour and 15 minutes, the chicken will be tender and golden brown. Serve with French fries (page 184) or with one of the spelt salads from page 209. A salad with preserved lemons like the one on page 118 also makes a delicious side dish.

RUBS

In our homemade barbecue and drum smoker in our garden in the south of France we make something different every day. Sometimes these projects take the whole day, sometimes just an hour or two.

Spare ribs, for example, can take some time to prepare, but once you've managed to tame the flames and the charcoal briquettes are glowing red, roasting the meat doesn't take too long. (In Amsterdam and Paris I don't have a garden, so I don't have a grill at home; naturally an oven at 350°F / 180°C works just as well.)

Dry rub seasonings (spice mixes) are very easy to make yourself. Just combine the spices and store them in an airtight container. Prepare a whole jar of your favorite mix so you'll only have to do it once per summer, and you'll have your meat ready in no time.

For both dry and wet rubs, first wash your hands meticulously and then thoroughly rub the seasoning into the meat, reaching every little nook and fold. Refrigerate the meat overnight, if you can, so the flavors can meld, but know that the impatients among us will consider it perfectly fine if it takes less time.

The quantities are enough for, say, five or six slabs of spare ribs.

Roast the spare ribs on a covered grill (use the lid or cover the meat loosely with a piece of aluminum foil) over a medium-hot fire for 2½ to 3 hours. You don't have to use any oil, as the meat has enough fat on its own.

If you roast your ribs in the oven, remove the foil for the last half hour of cooking.

joris's spicy rub

2 tbsp Chinese five-spice powder
(ground star anise, black pepper,
fennel seeds, cloves, and
cinnamon)

1 tbsp garlic powder
1 to 2 dried cayenne chiles
finely grated zest of 1½ lemons
1 tbsp turmeric

1 tbsp cardamom
plenty of salt and freshly ground
black pepper

my slightly sweeter rub

3 tbsp dark brown sugar
1 to 2 tbsp chile powder
2 tbsp dry mustard

2 tbsp curry powder
2 tbsp coriander seeds, ground in a
mortar

1 tbsp dried oregano
3 to 4 tbsp paprika
1 to 1½ tbsp salt

jalapeño & apple sauce

1⅔ cups (400 ml) organic apple
juice
1 to 2 tbsp minced jalapeño
1 tbsp finely grated fresh ginger
1 cup (250 ml) ketchup
3 tbsp red wine vinegar
2 tbsp Worcestershire sauce
1 tbsp dark brown sugar
3 tbsp ketjap manis (sweet soy sauce)
salt and freshly ground black pepper
2 tbsp chopped fresh cilantro or
chives

In a medium saucepan over medium-high heat, bring the apple juice, jalapeño, ginger, ketchup, vinegar, Worcestershire sauce, brown sugar, and ketjap manis to a boil and boil until the sauce is reduced by half. Season with salt and pepper to taste. Let cool completely, then stir in the cilantro.

Provence, France

Wim Bijma's neighbors, Amsterdam

gardianne de toro (beef stew)

I opened my book Home Made *with the "friendly" bull games from the French Camargue region. Nobody dies, nobody to be pitied, and after fifteen minutes the bulls are sent back to roam the vast nature reserve of the Camargue.*

Of course there are people who find this a form of animal cruelty as well, but I've seen these games two hundred times and though I'm a softy when it comes to animals, even I don't find it unpleasant.

It's truly a very exciting spectacle to see tough, athletic boys, who've practiced like crazy, performing all sorts of acrobatic maneuvers in order to fetch a string that is attached to the bull's horns. Those bulls are really wild and dangerous, so it's all about tactics and agility. Although the bulls roam freely in the nature reserve, the herd does belong to someone: a manadier, *or rancher. The game in which the teams of boys and the* manadiers *engage isn't just exciting, there's money to be made. Our friends from the south of France follow the sport closely, just as someone in the Netherlands might follow the national soccer league.*

Eventually old bulls will be eaten. Our friend Norbert makes an hourlong detour to drive to that one special butcher who sells the special bull beef.

Then he'll prepare us a gardianne de toro, *a beef stew that's traditionally eaten in the summer. By the way,* toro *is spelled correctly. The French may spell it* taureau, *but the southern* Provençao *use* toro.

FOR THE MARINADE

3 large onions, chopped

4 cloves garlic, minced

2 bay leaves

2 tbsp *quatre* épices (a mix of spices that can be bought everywhere in France, if you happen to be there; otherwise use a mix of ground black pepper, grated nutmeg, cloves, and cinnamon)

2 (750-ml) bottles of nice red wine

15 juniper berries, bruised in a mortar

a few sprigs of fresh thyme

salt to taste

AND FURTHER

6.5 lb (3 kg) bull, in chunks (although you will most likely end up using the more readily available beef stew meat)

olive oil for frying

3½ oz (100 g) bacon, diced

1 generous handful of all-purpose flour

1 generous handful of pitted black olives, such as kalamata, coarsely chopped if you wish

Make the marinade: In a large stockpot, combine all the ingredients and add the beef. Cover and let marinate in the refrigerator for 2 days, stirring occasionally.

Heat some oil over medium-high heat in a large, heavy cast-iron stew pot. Spoon the beef out of the marinade, reserving the marinade, and sear the beef in the pot, turning it until it is browned on all sides. I do this in two batches. Toward the end of the browning, add the bacon. Remove the meat from the pot.

Sprinkle the flour into the pot and cook it, stirring, until golden. Strain the marinade through a sieve, pour it into the pot, and stir until all the flour has been incorporated. Return the meat to the pot and bring everything to a boil. Lower the heat and let the stew simmer for 2 to 3 hours. Taste halfway through for salt and pepper. Add the olives at the very last moment. I'd recommend letting the *gardianne* cool, then refrigerating it for a day. Reheat and serve it the next day, when it will be at its most delicious.

Serve with Camargue rice, which speaks for itself.

Paluds de Noves

Norbert

Bas

Holysloot

BRAISED VEAL CHEEK
IN CLEAR CONSOMMÉ
WITH FRESH GREEN PEAS

IT TAKES A WHILE, BUT IT'S WELL WORTH IT

NOT THAT MUCH WORK, REALLY!

FIRST MAKE A CLEAR VEAL STOCK. IN MY BOOK HOME MADE YOU CAN FIND A FULL RECIPE FOR THIS, BUT HERE IS THE SHORT VERSION:

BROWN 1LB (500G) OF VEAL BONES (BUTCHER) + 2 SHANKS, 2 CHOPPED ONIONS, A BUNCH OF THYME, A BAY LEAF & GARLIC FOR ± 30 MIN.

PUT EVERYTHING IN A LARGE STOCKPOT & ADD 16 CUPS (4L) OF WATER, 1 WHOLE CELERY, 1 CARROT, PARSLEY, MACE, BLACK PEPPERCORNS, CORIANDER SEEDS AND 2 LEEKS → SLICED

BRING TO A BOIL, THEN LET IT COOK OVER VERY LOW HEAT FOR 3 HRS, OCCASIONALLY SKIMMING THE FOAM. STRAIN TROUGH A SIEVE LINED WITH A CLEAN DISH TOWEL, RETURN STOCK TO THE STOVE & SEASON.

THEN:

REMOVE THE MEMBRANE & ALL IRREGULAR PARTS FROM 14 OZ (400 G) OF VEAL CHEEK. (JUST DO IT, YOU'LL GET USED TO IT!)

CUT THE MEAT INTO 4 PARTS.

DUST WITH FLOUR, SALT & BLACK PEPPER & BROWN IN SOME BUTTER IN A SKILLET.

PUT THE MEAT IN THE HOT STOCK & STEW UNTIL TENDER: ABOUT 4 HRS OVER VERY LOW HEAT.

GO OFF TO THE GARDEN & PICK 2 HANDFULS OF GREEN PEAS, SOME FRESH MINT & MAYBE SOME FAVA BEANS. COOK AL DENTE.

SERVE THE VEAL CHEEK IN A BOWL WITH THE CONSOMMÉ & A HANDFUL OF THE VEGETABLES.
→ YOU'VE NEVER DINED THIS SUPERBLY.

Schellingwoude

MEAT

Joris

italian rib eyes with garlic and herbs

Or steaks, or pork chops, or chicken thighs, or roast beef, or drum sticks, or, or, or . . .

FOR THE MARINADE
10 cloves garlic, coarsely chopped
3 to 4 tbsp each of the following
    chopped fresh herbs: oregano,
    basil, parsley, and rosemary
1 tbsp salt
½ cup plus 2 tbsp (150 ml) olive oil
5 tbsp balsamic vinegar
2 tsp freshly ground white pepper

AND FURTHER
2 large boneless rib eyes, 10½ oz
    (300 g) each and at least 1 inch
    (2.5 cm) thick

Make the marinade: In a mortar or a mini food processor, mash the garlic together with the herbs and salt until you have a coarse paste. Stir in the oil, vinegar, and white pepper.

Set aside half of the mixture in a separate bowl.

Divide the other half between the steaks. Thoroughly rub it in with your hands. Set them aside to marinate for at least 1 hour.

Prepare a charcoal fire on an outdoor grill, or preheat a grill pan or skillet over medium heat and lightly oil the grill grate or pan.

Cook the rib eyes for 7 minutes, flip them over, and cook the other side for about 5 minutes, brushing both sides with the reserved marinade.

When you think they're done, remove the rib eyes from the heat. Let them sit for 15 minutes, covered loosely with aluminum foil; this way the juices can seep back into the meat. Cut the steak into strips and serve with a large salad.

BBQ TIP EXTRA ORDINAIRE!

SOAK A HANDFUL OF HARDWOOD CHIPS IN A BOWL OF WATER FOR 30 MINUTES OR SO. THESE CHIPS CAN BE BOUGHT AT MOST GOOD SUPERMARKETS AND AT HOME-IMPROVEMENT STORES. SPRINKLE THE HOT CHARCOAL BRIQUETTES WITH THE SOAKED WOOD CHIPS AND YOUR GRILLED MEAT WILL GET AN EVEN MORE DELICIOUS SMOKY FLAVOR → OH! (YOU CAN ALSO BUY WOODCHIPS MADE FROM OLD WHISKEY BARRELS !!!)

brined pork chops with sweet mustard barbecue sauce

4 thick bone-in pork chops, at least
    9 oz (250 g) each

FOR THE BRINE
¾ cup (250 g) salt
1¼ cups (250 g) sugar
1 tbsp juniper berries
4 to 6 bay leaves
1 tbsp fennel seed

FOR THE SWEET MUSTARD BARBECUE
    SAUCE
8 oz (200 g) prepared mustard,
    however strong or mild you
    prefer
⅓ cup (75 ml) red wine vinegar
⅓ cup (75 g) light brown sugar or
    granulated sugar
2 strong shots of brewed espresso
4 anchovy fillets
3 tbsp Worcestershire sauce
2 tsp Tabasco sauce

AND FURTHER, IF YOU WISH
4 tbsp hardwood chips for
    smoking, soaked for
    30 minutes

tip!

After brining, you can briefly smoke the cutlets, but it isn't *mandatory*, as the grill also adds a nice smoky flavor.

Trim the chops if necessary and set them aside.

Make the brine: In a medium saucepan, combine the salt and sugar with 4 cups (1 l) water, then add the juniper berries, bay leaves, and fennel. Bring to a boil, stirring until the salt and sugar are just about dissolved. Remove from the heat and let cool completely. Gently slide the meat into the brine, making sure it's totally submerged, and put it in the fridge overnight.

The next day, remove the chops from the brine and pat them dry with paper towels. Discard the brine. If you like, smoke the chops for 10 minutes in a smoker with the wood chips.

Make the sauce: Combine all the ingredients in a small saucepan and bring to a simmer. Add just enough water to make a nicely thick but pourable sauce and let it simmer until the anchovies are completely dissolved. If the sauce has reduced too much, add some more water. Remove it from the heat and set it aside in the pan until ready to use.

Prepare a charcoal fire in an outdoor grill, or preheat the oven. Briefly grill the chops on both sides, or roast them in the oven. Reheat the sauce if necessary on a vacant corner of the grill or on the stove. Serve the chops with the sauce on the side.

THAT'S A BRANDING-IRON GUN MADE BY MY FRIEND FRED. HOLD THE END IN THE GLOWING COALS & YOU CAN BRAND YOUR OWN MEAT. HOW COOL IS THAT?

·· MOLENKITCHEN ··

italian chicken stew with grilled goat cheese polenta

A favorite little recipe that gives you plenty of options. Even without the chicken, this dish works just fine. In that case supplement the stew with some extra mushrooms, or add more tomato and turn it into a soup. See, you can make this into whatever you want.

You can grate some fresh Parmesan over it, but a drizzle of olive oil is more than enough for me.

2 tbsp olive oil, plus more for serving
1 onion, diced
2 to 4 cloves garlic
1 or 2 dried hot red peppers
1 tbsp chopped fresh oregano
6 organic chicken thighs
salt and freshly ground black pepper
2 (14.5-oz/400-g) cans peeled
    tomatoes
2¼ lb (1 kg) thoroughly rinsed
    spinach, tough stems removed
4 ribs celery
handful of chanterelles

Heat the oil in a heavy skillet over medium heat and add the onion. Sauté for 2 minutes, until translucent, then add the garlic and crumble in the dried red peppers. Sauté briefly, then add the oregano. Season the chicken thighs with salt and pepper and place them in the skillet. Increase the heat to medium-high and brown both sides of the thighs. Pour in the tomatoes and add the spinach, celery, and mushrooms. Bring to a boil then reduce the heat to low and let the chicken stew for 45 minutes. Add salt and pepper to taste. Serve the stew with a generous drizzle of oil, and with polenta, rice, or mashed potatoes on the side, or simply in a large bowl with some rustic organic bread.

grilled goat cheese polenta

1 tbsp salt
2¼ cups (350 g) polenta
½ cup plus 2 tbsp (150 g) unsalted
    butter
6 oz (150 g) Chavroux or other
    creamy goat cheese
freshly ground black pepper

Bring 8 cups (2 l) water to a boil in a large saucepan. Add the salt. While whisking, use a measuring cup with a spout to gradually pour in the polenta in a thin trickle. If you don't pour gradually and whisk, the polenta will get lumpy and you'll have to start all over again.

Now the polenta starts bubbling like hot lava, but you remain unfazed and you lower the heat and you occasionally stir, until after 30 minutes the polenta is smooth and nicely thick. Add the butter and goat cheese and stir until everything is incorporated and the polenta is once again nice and smooth.

Give the pepper grinder a generous twist, then turn off the heat.

Grease a baking sheet or a shallow dish with oil and pour in the hot polenta. Let it cool completely. The polenta will now solidify.

Just before serving, heat a grill pan over medium heat and brush the surface with some oil. Cut the polenta into even triangles or rectangles and place them in the pan, one slice next to the other. Let them cook undisturbed for almost 10 minutes, then use a spatula to flip them when they have golden brown grill marks.

Serve the polenta with a saucy dish like the Italian stew above—but you surely will come up with some other delicious ideas as well.

crab legs with garlic butter

There is no escape: In Ireland you eat fish or shellfish. It's an island, after all. Not only is seafood readily available everywhere, but it's also of the highest quality.

I can hardly imagine a life without shellfish. Crab is among my favorites, and when I savored this wonderful little dish in Kenmare I immediately jotted it down in my notebook. It's so easy and ridiculously delicious that I'm certain it will become one of the staples of your summer repertoire.

Spread out some old newspapers on the kitchen table and encourage your family to eat with their hands. It'll become a bit of a mess, but you'll fold everything into the papers and in one fell swoop all will be nice and clean.

Eat this dish with some salad and bread—that's all.

FOR 4 SERVINGS
(OR 6 TO 8 AS A STARTER)

16 crab legs (you can buy these
     precooked at your local
     fishmonger)
5 tbsp (75 g) unsalted butter
⅓ cup (75 ml) nice olive oil
2 or 3 cloves garlic, minced
salt and freshly ground black pepper
handful of fresh flat-leaf parsley,
     chopped
½ handful of fresh tarragon (this
     is mandatory; make a detour if
     necessary)
1 lemon, quartered

Place the crab legs on a wooden cutting board and crush them somewhat using a hammer, just enough to allow the sauce to seep in, and also to make it easier to eat them.

Melt the butter in a large saucepan over medium heat, pour in the oil, and add the garlic. Season with salt and pepper and stir in the herbs.

Now add the crab legs; they probably won't all fit at once, so heat them in batches, turning them over in the butter so they become coated. (Heat the second batch while you devour the first.) Cover the pan and heat the crab legs for about 5 minutes, until they're heated through.

Spoon the crab legs out of the pan with a skimmer and transfer them to a large plate. Serve with the lemon wedges.

crab cakes with fresh citrus–tomato mayonnaise

When I think about America, I think about crab cakes. I don't know why. Well, it's probably because on our first visit, we made a road trip from New York up along the New England coast. We saw the largest lobsters ever, and we ate all of them. We ate all the oysters, too, and as soon as our appetite returned we'd order crab cakes. They were on every menu, so we didn't have to drive far to find them.

Like most people, when I got home I immediately wanted to make them myself, and it turns out there is nothing to it. Try it, and serve them with some salad, or eat them between two buns, like small burgers. You can grill them on a medium-hot barbecue or fry them—either way is delicious. Serve with a mild, fresh green salad.

FOR THE CRAB CAKES
1 tbsp unsalted butter
1 onion, diced
2 ribs celery, diced
about 6 oz (175 g) fresh crab meat,
 or 1 small can, drained
1¾ cups (200 g) bread crumbs
 (processing old bread yourself
 tastes best)
½ cup (125 ml) crème fraîche
a few fresh chives, minced
a few fresh basil leaves, minced
1 large egg
salt and freshly ground black pepper
light oil for frying

FOR THE MAYONNAISE
1 large egg yolk
juice of 1 lemon, or 2 tbsp vinegar
1 tbsp strong prepared mustard
about 2 cups (500 ml) sunflower or
 corn oil
2 tomatoes, seeded and diced
½ tsp paprika, preferably smoked
salt and freshly ground black pepper

Make the crab cakes: In a skillet over medium heat, melt the butter and sauté the onion and celery for about 4 minutes, until translucent. Transfer to a plate and let cool. Flake the crab meat into a bowl and add the cooled onion and celery, half of the bread crumbs, the crème fraîche, chives, basil, and egg, and season with salt and pepper. Stir to combine.

Shape the mixture into about 8 little balls. Slightly flatten them and coat the patties all over with the remaining bread crumbs.

In a nonstick sauté pan, heat some oil over medium heat. Fry the patties for about 2 minutes on each side, until golden brown on both sides. Let them drain on a paper towel.

Make the mayonnaise: In a food processor, combine the egg yolk, lemon juice, and mustard and process until foamy. With the motor running, pour in the oil in a very thin trickle until the mixture becomes a thick mayonnaise. By hand, stir in the tomatoes and paprika and season with salt and pepper. Serve with the crab cakes.

Graveson, 1982

la fête votive de st. eloi / de la madeleine

when we're in provence during summer, in the bouche du rhône (the mouth of the rhône river) to be precise, almost every day is a feast. in every village in the area there are grand feasts that, depending on the political color of the village, are called la fête de st. eloi or la fête votive de la madeleine.

it's a summer filled with processions in colorful traditional clothing and there's a fair (think: sixty years ago), there are performances, village breakfasts and banquets, and lots more.

the feasts adhere to a strict set of rules and traditions. every week it's a different village's turn to celebrate, and depending on how much money has been raised the festivities can become quite elaborate.

my favorite day is the day of the charette (the chariot). to improve the chances of a good harvest, the villagers decorate an old hay cart with flax, flowers, and vegetables. the chariot is pulled by a group of camargue horses with beautifully ornamented saddles ridden by boys cracking their whips. hidden inside the cart is a band that plays the same tune over and over again.

during the first passage through the streets, the horses (depending on the village funds, there can be a lot—between forty and eighty) will leisurely plod along, pulling the chariot, but with every lap the tempo is increased so that soon things get a little rough, up to a point where you can only hope that the hay cart and band will not swerve off the road.

in the end i often don't even dare to keep looking.

they like that, the french.

afterward we'll drink pastis with friends and family and we'll register for the grand banquet on the village square.

the menu never surprises: paella, aïoli, and moules frites, and that's about it.

the band on stage plays during the apéro, that lovely time that comes just before dinner, and elderly couples dance a little polka. these are the most wonderful evenings of your life.

moules frites

frites

Peel about 9 oz (250 g) potatoes per person. Cut them into
⅜-inch (1-cm) slices and then cut those slices into ⅜-inch (1-cm)
strips. Put them in ice-cold water to wash off any excess starch,
so they'll get more crunchy when you cook them. Drain and
thoroughly pat them dry with a clean dish towel.

You'll fry the potatoes twice. First heat a good amount of oil
(6 inches/15 cm deep) in a large pot or deep-fryer to 325°F
(160°C). Fry one generous handful of fries at a time. Not all
at once, or the oil will cool down too fast and your fries will be
soggy. Fry for about 6 minutes, allowing the inside to pre-cook
a bit, occasionally flipping them over with a skimmer. At this
point they shouldn't brown; they should remain pale. Scoop
them out and let them cool and drain for at least 30 minutes on
some paper towels. You can do this a day in advance; keep them
covered in the fridge until ready to use, and leave the oil, covered,
in the pot or deep-fryer.

When ready to serve, heat the same oil to 375°F (190°C) and again
fry the fries in small batches, this time until they become golden
brown and crisp. This should take 3 to 4 minutes per batch.

Sprinkle with some sea salt and serve immediately.

moules à la moutarde et au pastis

9 lb (4 kg) mussels
4 large onions, minced
4 large shallots, minced
1 celery rib, minced
4 to 6 cloves garlic, passed through a
    garlic press
375 ml (½ bottle) white wine
6 tbsp strong prepared mustard
¾ cup (200 ml) heavy cream
1 bunch fresh flat-leaf parsley, finely
    chopped
¾ cup (200 ml) pastis (Pernod or
    Ricard)
salt and freshly ground black pepper

Wash the mussels in a pan or bowl filled with cold water and
carefully look for mussels that don't close when you tap them
(which means they're dead) or that have crushed shells. Throw
these out.

Place a large pot on the stove and add the onions, shallots, celery,
and garlic and the wine. Stir in the mustard and bring to a boil
over medium-high heat. Lower the heat to low and cook for about
15 minutes, until the vegetables are softened. Turn the heat back
up, stir in the cream, and when it starts boiling fiercely add the
mussels. Cover the pot, but once in a while scoop the mussels
around until all of them have opened (discard any that do not
open). Add the parsley and pastis and season with salt and pepper.

Serve with *frites*.

Clovis

Magali

185

cedar–smoked apple salmon

Browsing for new ideas online, I noticed that smoking fish on a cedar roasting plank is becoming pretty popular in the United States. Naturally I wanted to try this too.

The result, it turned out, was amazing. Soak a food-safe cedar plank in water (don't get one from the lumber yard, as it may have been treated with chemicals; use the ones you find in grocery stores and near the grilling supplies in home-improvement stores), put a piece of fish on it, and grill the whole thing. You can place the plank directly on the embers, but your cedar won't be reusable. To get more uses from your plank, place it on top of the grill grate, or in your oven.

1 cedar roasting plank, about 12 x 16 inches (30 x 40 cm)

1¼ cups (300 ml) hard apple cider, or ¾ cup (200 ml) organic apple juice and ⅓ cup plus 1 tbsp (100 ml) apple cider vinegar

3 scallions, thinly sliced

1 tbsp salt

1 tbsp grated fresh ginger

1 clove garlic, passed through a garlic press

2 lb (1 kg) salmon fillet, skin removed

Soak the plank in water for at least 1 hour, but preferably longer. In a shallow dish, combine the cider, scallions, salt, ginger, and garlic. Place the salmon fillet in the marinade, making sure both sides are thoroughly coated. Cover the dish and let the salmon marinate for at least 1 hour, but overnight in the refrigerator is even better. The salmon will become tender.

Prepare a medium-hot charcoal fire in an outdoor grill and wait until all the briquettes are covered with a layer of ash, and the fire only gently smolders.

Remove the fish from the marinade and transfer it to the cedar plank. Put the plank on the grill grate or directly on the smoldering ashes. Cover the plank with aluminum foil and cook for 10 to 20 minutes, depending on how well-done you like your salmon and the thickness of the fillet. You know, you can eat salmon raw, so I'd say don't leave it on too long.

If the wood catches fire, douse it with some water—a spray bottle comes in handy.

Eat the salmon straight away, with a nice large salad.

Instant bliss.

baby squid à la horas

Like me, my dear friend Horas runs a small restaurant and a catering service. His are in the Hague. We regularly exchange tips and ideas, because that's how it goes among friends who are in the same profession.

Horas was so excited about this recipe that he sent it to me straight away. I tried it out and . . . he was right, it's amazing.

It's really not much work at all, with hardly any ingredients, and the flavors immediately remind you of summer vacation. Eat it with bread, to soak up the sauce, or with pasta—linguine, for example. Make a quick green salad to go alongside, and you have the ultimate summer meal.

2 lb (1 kg) baby squid, cleaned (you can also use baby octopus)
1 hot red or green chile, sliced
splash of olive oil
salt and coarsely ground black pepper
lemon wedges
1 tsp unsalted butter
2 tbsp chopped fresh parsley

Preheat the oven to 200°F (100°C). Spread the squid and chile in a roasting pan or baking dish with a lid, drizzle with oil, and season with salt and pepper. Cover the pan and bake for about 2 hours while you go lounge in the sun, until the squid is tender when you pierce one with a fork. Squeeze some lemon juice over them. Stir the butter into the warm pan and sprinkle everything with parsley. Eat warm straight from the oven, or serve at room temperature.

sea bass fillets with crouton crust and a fennel salad

3 or 4 slices stale white bread
1 cup (100 g) grated Pecorino or
    Parmesan cheese
pinch of cayenne
1 tbsp chopped fresh oregano, or
    ½ tbsp dried
1 clove garlic, passed through a garlic
    press
grated zest of ½ lemon
2 anchovy fillets, minced
2 tbsp olive oil, plus more for the
    baking sheet
4 sea bass fillets, with skin

AS A SIDE DISH
2 small bulbs fennel, tough outer
    layer removed
handful of arugula
a few fresh chives, coarsely chopped
juice of 1 lemon
⅓ cup plus 2 tbsp (100 ml) olive oil
salt and freshly ground black pepper

OPTIONAL
A handful of alfalfa sprouts

Preheat the oven to 325°F (160°C).

Finely dice the bread. Spread it on a baking sheet and bake for about 20 minutes, until dry and light brown. Remove from the oven and increase the oven temperature to 350°F (180°C).

Transfer the croutons to a bowl and toss with the cheese, cayenne, oregano, garlic, lemon zest, anchovies, and oil.

Oil a baking sheet and place the fish on it, skin side up. Arrange the crouton mixture on top of the fillets and bake in the center of the oven for 8 minutes—tops.

Meanwhile, make a salad: Slice the fennel as thinly as possible.

Toss with the arugula and chives. Drizzle some lemon juice and oil on top and sprinkle with salt and pepper.

Serve with the fish.

pasta shells with spring greens, mâche, and prosciutto

FOR 4 TO 6 SERVINGS

2 tbsp unsalted butter

2 tbsp extra-virgin olive oil, plus
more for serving

1 large shallot, diced

coarse sea salt and freshly ground
black pepper

⅓ cup plus 2 tbsp (100 ml) dry white
wine

⅓ cup plus 2 tbsp (100 ml) chicken
stock

1 bunch asparagus, trimmed and cut
on a diagonal into 1- to 1½-inch
(3- to 4-cm) pieces

7 oz (200 g) fresh green shelled peas

1 lb (500 g) dried pasta shells

1 head of mâche (corn salad),
smaller leaves left whole, larger
leaves torn

1½ cups (150 g) grated Parmesan
cheese, plus more for serving

3 tbsp chopped fresh flat-leaf
parsley

7 oz (200 g) thinly sliced prosciutto,
cut diagonally into strips

Melt the butter with the oil in a large skillet over low heat. Add the shallot and season with coarse salt and pepper. Sauté over low heat, for 7 to 8 minutes, until soft but not browned. Add the wine, increase the heat, and boil for about 3 minutes. Add the stock and bring to a boil.

Remove from the heat and set aside.

Bring a large saucepan of salted water to a boil and add the asparagus. Boil for 2 to 4 minutes (depending on the thickness of your asparagus), until al dente. Remove the asparagus with a skimmer and transfer them to a bowl of ice water. Add the peas to the boiling water and boil for 2 minutes, until al dente. Use the skimmer to transfer them to the ice water.

Add the pasta to the boiling water and cook until al dente. Reserve ¾ cup (200 ml) of the cooking liquid and drain the pasta in a colander.

Reheat the pan containing the sautéed shallots. Add the mâche and toss for about 1 minute, until it begins to wilt. Drain the asparagus and peas and add them to the pan just to heat through.

Add the pasta, sprinkle with Parmesan and parsley, and toss to heat through. If the sauce is too dry, add some of the reserved cooking liquid. Season with salt and pepper.

Transfer to a large shallow bowl. Sprinkle with the prosciutto and drizzle with oil. Serve with some extra Parmesan—what a joy!

quinoa patties with feta, zucchini, and corn

FOR ABOUT 10 PATTIES: 1 CUP (175 G) COOKED QUINOA • 2 EGGS, BEATEN • PINCH OF SALT •
2½ TBSP (15 G) MINCED FRESH CHIVES AND PARSLEY (MIXED) • ½ ZUCCHINI,
COARSELY GRATED • KERNELS FROM 1 EAR OF CORN • 1 SMALL SHALLOT, DICED • 1 CLOVE GARLIC, MINCED •
1 TSP PAPRIKA • PINCH OF CAYENNE OR RED PEPPER FLAKES • ½ TSP BAKING POWDER • ¾ CUP (75 G) BREAD
CRUMBS, OR MORE IF NECESSARY • ⅔ CUP (75 G) CRUMBLED FETA • OLIVE OIL FOR FRYING

PREHEAT THE OVEN TO 350°F (180°C).

IN A BOWL, COMBINE THE QUINOA, EGGS, SALT, CHIVES AND PARSLEY,
ZUCCHINI, CORN, SHALLOT, GARLIC, PAPRIKA, AND CAYENNE.

ADD THE BAKING POWDER AND THE BREAD CRUMBS AND LET THE MIXTURE STAND FOR ABOUT 10 MINUTES,
SO THE CRUMBS CAN ABSORB SOME OF THE LIQUID. THEN STIR IN THE FETA.

HEAT A SHALLOW LAYER OF OIL IN A SKILLET. USING TWO TEASPOONS, MAKE SMALL BALLS FROM THE QUINOA MIXTURE
AND FRY THE PATTIES OR BALLS FOR 2 TO 3 MINUTES ON EACH SIDE, FLIPPING THEM TO BROWN THEM ON ALL SIDES.

EAT THE PATTIES AS A MEAT REPLACEMENT WITH VEGETABLES, OR AS A SNACK
WITH DIPPING SAUCE—THE YOGURT DIP WITH MINT ON PAGE 175, FOR EXAMPLE.

THIS IS HOW YOU COOK QUINOA:

RINSE THE QUINOA WELL IN A SIEVE. BRING A LARGE SAUCEPAN OF SALTED WATER TO A BOIL.
ADD THE QUINOA. SET YOUR TIMER FOR 10 MINUTES. AS SOON AS THE TIME IS UP,
DRAIN THE QUINOA IN THE SIEVE AND RINSE WITH COLD WATER.

Carmargue, France

buttery corn risotto

There's nothing more summery than crisp, buttery sweet corn. In our restaurant we have cooks who hate corn and cooks who love it near-unconditionally. I'm in the latter group. The Parmesan and the extra butter added to the risotto at the end of cooking—a technique called mantecura—*make it especially rich. I could honestly eat the whole pan myself. It's great on its own, or with pork or roast chicken.*

4 ears sweet corn, shucked

2 leeks

½ rib celery

1 tbsp coriander seeds

1 bay leaf

bouquet garni: a few sprigs of fresh parsley, thyme, and, if you wish, tarragon, tied together with kitchen string

1 or 2 shallots, diced

1 tbsp unsalted butter

2½ cups (250 g) risotto rice (Vialone Nano or Arborio)

1 glass dry white vermouth (about 150–200 ml; it will evaporate)

1 small bunch flat-leaf parsley, minced

¾ cup (75 g) grated Parmesan cheese

In a large saucepan, combine the corn, leeks, celery, coriander, bay leaf, and bouquet garni and cover with water. Simmer gently for 30 minutes over low heat. Remove the corn with tongs and strain the stock through a sieve into a bowl, discarding the solids. Cut the corn kernels from the cobs.

In a large skillet, sauté the shallots with 1 tbsp of the butter until soft, then add the rice and cook until the rice grains are translucent. Add the vermouth and then add a ladleful of the corn stock. Stir until the rice has absorbed most of the liquid. Continue in this manner, adding stock a ladleful at a time, stirring constantly, until the risotto is creamy and the rice is al dente. Add the corn kernels, chopped parsley, the remaining butter, and the cheese. Stir, remove from the heat, cover, and let the butter melt. Serve hot.

Georges, king of the vegetable garden

bohemièn à la georges

When we arrive at the farm of the brothers Georges and Charles in Provence, they always hand us a glass of pastis, whatever time of day it is.

Then we go to the terrace or the kitchen if it's too hot, and we catch up on all the village and family gossip. Then we immediately make a dinner date.

Georges and Charles always cook the same meal for their guests. That's because Georges makes the best bohemièn *in the south of France. As soon as he begins his preparations for the dish he starts giving us updates on how it's going: that he tasted it and that, of course, it's even more delicious than the last time we ate it.*

Bohemièn resembles ratatouille, but with only eggplant and tomato as the main ingredients. The trick is to *stew it gently and slowly and to let it rest for a while before you serve it.*

So begin cooking in the morning, do some gardening or something, then come back to it that night.

Eat it with caillettes *(meatballs) or with a bean salad and bread.*

Georges makes it a tad sweeter than I do, but other than that, this is his recipe.

4 eggplants, diced
salt
½ cup plus 2 tbsp (150 ml) olive oil
4½ lb (2 kg) good tomatoes, diced
4 cloves garlic, minced
a handful of fresh parsley, chopped
2 tsp sugar
freshly ground black pepper

Sprinkle the eggplant with salt and let it sit in the refrigerator overnight or for an afternoon. Rinse it and squeeze it dry.

Heat the oil in a heavy cast-iron skillet over medium heat and add the eggplant; cook, stirring occasionally, until lightly browned. Reduce the heat to low, add the tomatoes and garlic, and cook for at least 2 hours. Remove from the heat and add the parsley and sugar. Season with salt and pepper. Let cool.

Reheat the dish just before serving.

You can easily make this a day in advance, so it's a great meal for a barbecue or party.

birthday

my mother's birthday is in may. when her mother was still alive, for the occasion she would take the train all the way from limburg, a southern province in the netherlands, to visit us. my sister and i would pick her up from track 8 at the haarlem train station.

in a big bag, wrapped in a wet towel, was my mother's present: a giant heap of white asparagus, fresh from the farm, and already peeled. (that's what made it so presentlike.) "the asparagus should squeak like guinea pigs when they move alongside each other in the towel," said my grandmother: that's how you know they're fresh.

the tradition continued. though my mother doesn't travel all the way to limburg to buy asparagus, we do eat them on her birthday.

if it's nice out we'll eat in the garden: classic asparagus, with ham, eggs, parsley, a butter sauce, and new potatoes.

for dessert we'll have strawberries with cream.

the next day we eat asparagus soup, made from the previous day's asparagus peelings and cooking liquid.

my grandmother's white asparagus, limburg style

Count on about 12 oz (350 g) asparagus per person if you serve them with ham, and a little more if you serve them without. Peel the lower two thirds or so of the asparagus with a vegetable peeler, and make sure you peel it thoroughly or you'll find yourself eating the strings later. Cut off the tough ends. Keep the trimmings, as you can use them for asparagus soup the next day.

FOR EACH PERSON, ADD THE
FOLLOWING TO A LARGE
SAUCEPAN OF BOILING WATER:

1 piece mace
1 tsp sugar (yes, really!)
½ tsp salt

Add the asparagus. You should adapt the cooking time depending on how you'll use the asparagus. If I'm using it in a salad I like it quite firm, and I'll cook it for just 8 to 10 minutes. If I'm eating it as a main vegetable, I like to cook it for 25 minutes, so it's softer. The latter is what my mother and grandmother did—they never prepare them otherwise. Use a skimmer to remove the asparagus from the water and let it drain on a clean dish towel.

For the soup, put the asparagus peels and hard ends in the cooking liquid and cook them for 1 hour or so over low heat. You can do this while you're eating or you can do it the next day. See further soup directions below.

serve the asparagus with the following

FOR 4 SERVINGS

7 tbsp (100 g) unsalted butter, at
    room temperature
4 small eggs
12 oz (350 g) organic ham (the best
    you can find), thinly sliced
1 small bunch fresh tarragon (15 g),
    finely chopped
finely grated zest of ½ lemon
1 tsp flaky salt
freshly ground black pepper

Melt the butter in a small saucepan over low heat and separate the clear part from the white solids, reserving the clear part on a hot plate to keep it warm. This is called clarifying the butter. (You can throw out the white solids.)

Put the eggs in a small saucepan, cover with water, and bring to a boil. As soon as the water boils, set the timer to 3 minutes. When done, drain and immediately rinse the eggs under cold running water to cool them; this will make peeling easier. Peel the eggs and cut them in half with a sharp knife. For each person, wrap a bunch of asparagus (keep them warm on a hot plate under a clean towel until you have finished the rest) in 2 slices of the ham. You can wrap a sprig of tarragon around them, just for fun, because it looks so pretty. Place each asparagus bunch on a warm plate with 2 egg halves. Pour some clarified butter over the asparagus. Sprinkle with lemon zest, salt, and pepper.

My grandmother would serve them with boiled new potatoes in their skins, which is terrific. But I serve them with little soufflés (foolproof ones that you can make in advance). You'll find the recipe on page 205.

my foolproof double–baked tarragon soufflés

FOR 6 SOUFFLÉS

5 tbsp (75 g) unsalted butter, plus
    more for greasing
½ cup plus 2 tbsp (75 g) all-purpose
    flour
2 cups (500 ml) milk
pinch of freshly grated nutmeg
salt and freshly ground black pepper
6 large eggs, separated
1½ cups (150 g) grated Parmesan
    cheese
1 tsp chopped fresh tarragon
½ cup plus 2 tbsp (150 ml) heavy
    cream (if reheating the soufflés)

Preheat the oven to 350°F (180°C). Place 6 individual-size soufflé dishes in a large roasting pan or deep lasagna dish and fill the pan with hot water to reach three quarters of the way up the sides of the dishes. Remove the dishes from the pan and place the pat in the center of the oven. Butter the soufflé dishes. In a heavy saucepan over medium heat, melt the butter with the flour to make a paste, or roux. Cook the roux for a few minutes, stirring, so the flour loses its raw taste, then stir in the milk. Bring to a boil, stirring well, and cook just until the sauce begins to thicken, then remove the pan from the heat. Add the nutmeg, and season with salt and pepper. Stir in the egg yolks, then the cheese and tarragon. Set aside.

In a clean bowl, beat the egg whites with a pinch of salt until stiff. Gently fold the egg whites into the egg-cheese mixture. Divide the batter among the prepared soufflé dishes and place them in the roasting pan of hot water. Bake for 20 minutes, until golden brown. Remove the dishes from the pan of water and let them cool for a bit, then gently tip the soufflés out of the dishes.

Serve right away, with the asparagus, or place them upside down on a baking sheet to cool completely. You can also keep them in the fridge, covered, overnight. When you're ready to serve them, preheat the oven to 400°F (200°C). Dip the tops of the soufflés in some cream, let the cream drip down along the sides, it doesn't matter, and arrange them on a baking sheet. Bake for about 7 minutes, or until they are nicely puffy and soufflé-y again. Serve.

and more asparagus tips!

* Arrange lightly cooked asparagus on a bruschetta of sourdough bread with ricotta, chervil, and a poached egg (see page 28) and some sautéed morels, if you wish.

* A salad with near-raw asparagus is also lovely; cut the spears on a diagonal into thirds and toss them in an herb salad (see page 28).

* Make asparagus soup. This is a basic recipe; you can improvise a lot. In a medium saucepan over medium heat, melt 3 tbsp (40 g) unsalted butter with ⅓ cup (40 g) all-purpose flour. Cook the roux for a few minutes. Stir in 4 cups (1 l) of asparagus cooking liquid (made from the peelings) and a few pieces of cooked asparagus. Boil the soup down for about 20 minutes, and stir in ⅓ cup plus 2 tsp (100 ml) milk and ⅓ cup plus 2 tsp (100 ml) heavy cream. Boil the soup down until it has the desired thickness. Season with nutmeg, salt, and pepper. Serve with lots of parsley or tarragon and a handful of croutons.

tatin of eggplant, red onion, and pine nuts

This is a main course, but it could also be a lunch dish, or an in-between meal. Usually I need to stop myself from going into the kitchen again and again to sneak another slice. It's that good.

FOR THE SHORTCRUST DOUGH
2½ cups (300 g) all-purpose flour
pinch of salt
½ cup plus 2 tbsp (150 g) unsalted
     butter, cut into chunks
1 large egg yolk
1 tbsp fresh thyme leaves

FOR THE FILLING
2 eggplants
olive oil
salt and freshly ground black pepper
4 red onions
2 tbsp sugar
2 tbsp pine nuts
1 tbsp chopped fresh sage
⅔ cup (75 g) crumbled feta

Make the shortcrust dough. Combine the flour, salt, and butter in a food processor and pulse a few times until you have coarse crumbs. Add the egg yolk and thyme and pulse a few more times. Add a few drops of ice-cold water and pulse a few times until the dough just sticks together. The secret of a nice tender crust is working quickly and kneading only briefly. Wrap the dough in plastic wrap and chill in the fridge for 1 hour.

Preheat the oven to 350°F (180°C).

Slice the eggplants into ¼-inch (½-cm) slices. Generously oil one or two baking sheets and arrange the eggplant slices in them in a single layer. Sprinkle both sides of the slices with salt and pepper. Bake for 20 to 25 minutes, until they are light brown. Flip the slices after about 15 minutes, so both sides brown.

Meanwhile, cut the onions into rounds and sauté them gently in oil until they are tender; season with salt and pepper and stir occasionally.

Cut a piece of parchment paper the size of a springform pan. Pour some oil in the pan, place the parchment paper on the bottom, and oil the paper and the sides of the pan. Sprinkle the bottom with the sugar and pine nuts. Cover the bottom with overlapping eggplant slices and onion rings and scatter the sage in between.

Roll out the dough on a floured counter into a circle the size of the pan. Place the dough on top of the vegetables in the pan and tuck in the edges. Make a hole in the middle of the dough to allow steam to escape.

Bake the tatin for 35 minutes, until the crust is golden brown and the vegetables are caramelized.

Let the tatin rest on the counter for 5 minutes. Remove the sides of the springform pan and invert the tart onto a large plate.

Sprinkle with crumbled feta and serve immediately.

Mediterranean Salad

Barcelona

Barcelona

Spelt Salad

mediterranean salad with spelt, eggplant, zucchini & marinated cheese

FOR THE MARINATED CHEESE
5 oz (150 g) ricotta salata or
    Pecorino cheese
1 tsp red pepper flakes
⅓ cup (75 ml) extra-virgin olive oil

FOR THE SALAD
2 eggplants, diced
2 zucchini, diced
5 tbsp olive oil
1 tsp salt
freshly ground black pepper
¾ cup (100 g) spelt (soaked in water
    for 1 hour if you wish)
1 pint tasty cherry tomatoes,
    quartered
¾ cup (100 g) kalamata or other
    salty black olives, pitted
¼ cup coarsely chopped mint leaves

FOR THE DRESSING
juice of 1 lemon
½ tsp coriander
½ tsp paprika
1 tsp sugar
⅓ cup plus 2 tbsp (100 ml) extra-
    virgin olive oil

Preheat the oven to 350°F (180°C).

Make the marinated cheese: Put the cheese and red pepper flakes in a bowl and pour the oil over them. Let marinate for at least 1 hour.

Make the salad: Arrange the eggplant and zucchini on a baking sheet and sprinkle with the oil and salt. Season with pepper. Toss well and bake for about 30 minutes, until light brown, turning the vegetables over halfway through. Remove them from the oven and transfer them to a large bowl.

Meanwhile, cook the spelt in a large saucepan of boiling water with a pinch of salt until al dente. If you've soaked the spelt first it should be ready after about 20 minutes; otherwise it will need more time, between 30 and 40 minutes. Drain the spelt in a sieve and rinse under cold running water; drain well.

Make the dressing: In a small bowl, whisk together the lemon juice, coriander, paprika, and sugar, then trickle in the oil, whisking until it emulsifies. Add the spelt, tomatoes, and olives to the bowl with the eggplant and zucchini. Toss everything and drizzle the dressing on top. Let the salad stand for 1 hour, to allow the various flavors to be absorbed.

Serve, garnished with slivers of the marinated cheese and sprinkled with mint leaves.

spelt salad with sweet–tart beets

1½ cups (200 g) spelt
10 oz (300 g) cooked beets, peeled
    and cubed
1 bunch watercress
1 carrot

FOR THE DRESSING
⅓ cup (75 ml) raspberry vinegar
2 to 3 tbsp golden syrup
1 tbsp prepared mustard
salt and freshly ground black pepper
½ cup (125 ml) light vegetable oil
3½ tbsp (50 ml) walnut oil

Cook the spelt in a large saucepan of salted boiling water until tender, about 35 minutes. Drain in a sieve and rinse under cold running water; drain well.

Make the dressing: In a large bowl, whisk the vinegar, syrup, and mustard together and season with salt and pepper.

Add the oils in a thin trickle, whisking constantly until the dressing emulsifies.

Add the beets and spelt to the dressing and set aside until ready to serve.

Cut off the stems from the watercress and wash the leaves. Dry the watercress in a salad spinner. Peel the carrot and slice as thinly as possible, then add the carrot and watercress to the spelt-beet salad just before serving. Toss and serve immediately.

salad with fennel, dates, and parmesan (or comté) with walnut dressing

Serve with a crackling dry white wine.

FOR THE SALAD

3 ribs celery, very thinly sliced on the diagonal
1 bulb fennel, cleaned, cut in half vertically, and very thinly sliced
juice of ½ lemon
handful of fresh flat-leaf parsley
3 tbsp hulled pumpkin seeds, briefly toasted in a dry skillet
5 oz (150 g) Parmesan or aged Comté cheese, cut into julienne
10 dates, pitted and cut into julienne
a handful of walnut halves, toasted

FOR THE DRESSING

juice of ½ lemon
2 tbsp olive oil
2 tbsp walnut oil
salt and freshly ground black pepper

Make the salad: Combine the celery and fennel in a bowl and toss with the lemon juice to prevent discoloring. Add all the remaining ingredients and toss well.

Make the dressing: Put the lemon juice in a small bowl and whisk in the oils in a thin trickle; season with salt and pepper. Pour the dressing over the salad, toss well, and serve immediately.

rolled–up feta & garlic bread with radicchio and mint

FOR THE DOUGH
1 (¼-oz/7-g) envelope active dry
    yeast
1¼ cups (300 ml) lukewarm milk
1 tbsp sugar
3 tbsp olive oil, plus more for the pan
4 cups (500 g) all-purpose flour
generous pinch of salt

FOR THE FILLING
½ cup plus 6 tbsp (200 g) unsalted
    butter, at room temperature
2 small cloves garlic, minced
3 tbsp minced fresh mint
freshly ground black pepper and
    perhaps a pinch of salt
generous handful of sliced radicchio
⅔ cup (75 g) crumbled feta cheese

Make the dough: In a small bowl, combine the yeast with the warm milk, sugar, and oil and set aside for 5 minutes until the yeast dissolves. In a large bowl, combine the flour and salt. While mixing, pour in the milk mixture. Make sure all the yeast comes along with it!

Transfer the dough to a lightly floured counter and knead the dough until you have a nice supple smooth ball that is no longer sticky. You might have to add a little more flour.

Place the dough in a bowl and cover with plastic wrap.

Let rise for 1 hour.

Make the filling: With an electric mixer, beat the butter until creamy. Add the garlic, mint, and pepper and beat well. You can add some salt if you wish, but remember that the feta is salty, so be judicious. Cover and set aside.

Blanch the radicchio in boiling water for 2 seconds and drain well in a sieve. Chop it even more finely.

Preheat the oven to 350°F (180°C). Oil a 9-inch (24-cm) round baking dish, tart pan, or springform pan.

Knead the dough briefly, then dust the counter with flour, shape the dough into a rectangle, and roll it out into a large rectangle about 16 x 20 inches (40 x 50 cm).

Reserve about one quarter of the garlic butter, and spread the remaining garlic butter over the dough. Sprinkle with the feta. Roll up the dough from the long side and wrap it in plastic wrap. Place the roll in the freezer for about 15 minutes to stiffen; cutting will be easier that way. Melt the reserved garlic butter in a saucepan and remove from the heat.

Cut the roll into 1- to 1½-inch (3- to 4-cm) slices. Arrange them close together in the baking dish; it's fine if they touch each other. Brush the tops with the melted garlic butter and let stand for another 15 minutes. Bake for about 30 minutes, until golden brown. *Delicious.*

spicy ratatouille

generous splash of good olive oil
2 large onions, sliced into rounds
2 cloves garlic, minced
½ red bell pepper, coarsely chopped
½ green bell pepper, coarsely
    chopped
1 zucchini, diced
1 eggplant, diced
4 nice big tomatoes, coarsely
    chopped
1 tbsp chopped fresh thyme
1 tbsp harissa, or to taste
salt and freshly ground black pepper
3 tbsp chopped fresh parsley

Heat the oil in a heavy skillet over medium heat. Add the onions and sauté for a few minutes, until soft and light brown, then add the garlic and sauté for 1 minute. Add all the remaining ingredients except the parsley, reduce the heat to low, and cook for about 30 minutes, until the vegetables are nicely tender.

Sprinkle with the parsley and drizzle with a little more oil just before serving.

large polenta pizza with ratatouille

olive oil for the pan
1 tbsp salt, or more to taste
1¼ cups (200 g) polenta
3 tbsp (50 g) butter
1¼ cups (75 g) freshly grated
    Parmesan
freshly ground black pepper
1 recipe ratatouille (above), cooled

Oil a large (12-inch / 30-cm) round cake pan or baking dish. Add the salt to 4 cups (1 l) water in a large saucepan and bring to a boil over high heat. Pour in the polenta in a thin stream, stirring constantly until smooth (be careful: polenta splatters terribly). Reduce the heat to low and cook, stirring frequently to make sure the polenta doesn't get lumpy, for about 30 minutes, until the polenta is thick. If you see a lump, stir vigorously until it dissolves. Add the butter and ¾ cup of the Parmesan and stir until all is absorbed. Taste for salt and pepper.

Pour the polenta into the cake pan or baking dish. Use the back of a spoon dipped in water to smooth out the polenta. Let cool completely and solidify.

Preheat the oven to 350°F (180°C).

Top the polenta with the cooled ratatouille, leaving a little space around the perimeter. Sprinkle with the remaining Parmesan and bake for 25 minutes, until the edges start to brown.

Serve as part of a main course with grilled meat, like the ribs on page 164, or grilled fish, or serve it with a green salad as a light lunch.

215

Paris

Amsterdam

216

small potatoes with sauce gribiche

Usually you'll have all the ingredients you need for this at home, so it's easy. Open your fridge and check. If you don't have fennel, feel free to leave it out; it's my own addition because I like it a lot, but it's certainly not necessary.

2 large eggs, plus 1 egg yolk
1 lb (500 g) small potatoes
2 tbsp (25 g) unsalted butter
½ cup (125 ml) light olive oil
1 tbsp strong prepared mustard
2 tbsp red wine vinegar
salt and freshly ground black pepper
8 cornichons, chopped
2 tbsp drained capers
½ bulb fennel, finely diced
1 bunch (20 g) fresh flat-leaf parsley,
    chopped

Boil the whole eggs for 10 minutes. Drain and rinse thoroughly under cold running water. Peel them and set aside in a small bowl of water until ready to use. At the same time, boil the potatoes for 10 minutes, until they're not quite tender. Drain them too and rinse under cold water. Drain thoroughly.

Heat the butter and 2 tbsp (25 ml) of the oil in a skillet over medium heat and fry the potatoes until crisp and golden brown, stirring constantly.

In a small saucepan over medium heat, combine the mustard and vinegar and stir just until hot. Remove the pan from the heat and quickly stir in the egg yolk. While stirring, pour in the remaining oil, and continue to stir until you have a smooth sauce. Halve the boiled eggs, flip out the hard-boiled yolks, and mash them into the sauce as well. Season with salt and pepper. Add the cornichons, capers, fennel, and parsley. Coarsely chop the hard-boiled egg whites and toss them in.

Put the potatoes in a large bowl and mix with a generous amount of the sauce (you might not need it all). Serve immediately. And by the way, *sauce gribiche* is also delicious on cold cuts, asparagus, or fish.

mashed potatoes with fresh green herbs and lemon

2 lb (1 kg) russet potatoes, peeled
½ cup (125 ml) heavy cream, plus
    more if necessary
about 5 tbsp (75 g) unsalted butter,
    cut into pieces, plus more for
    the baking dish
5 tbsp finely chopped fresh herbs:
    tarragon, dill, and flat-leaf
    parsley
grated zest and juice of 1 lemon
pinch of freshly grated nutmeg
salt and freshly ground black pepper
2 or 3 scallions, sliced
1 large egg, beaten (if baking the
    mashed potatoes)

If you'd like to bake the mashed potatoes, preheat the oven to 350°F (180°C) and generously butter a baking dish.

Chop the potatoes and cook them in a large pan of boiling salted water until very tender. Drain. Mash with a masher, or preferably, pass through a potato ricer. *Never* use an immersion blender or electric mixer; the puree will become tough and slimy, and that's simply gross.

Add the cream a little at a time; you may not need all of it; just stop adding when you think the mash is just right for you and not too wet. Add the butter. Stir in the herbs, lemon zest and juice, and nutmeg. Season with salt and pepper.

Serve garnished with the scallions.

If you are baking the potatoes, stir in the egg (so the potatoes puff up a little in the oven, like a soufflé) and spoon the potatoes into the baking dish.

Bake for 10 minutes, until it's nicely puffed up and golden brown. Serve garnished with the scallions.

Meanwhile, on the canals in Amsterdam . . .

Meanwhile, in Sophie's garden . . .

Provence, France

lemon or pink grapefruit tart with meringue

FOR THE DOUGH
2½ cups (300 g) all-purpose flour
pinch of salt
2 tbsp sugar
½ cup plus 2 tbsp (150 g) cold
    unsalted butter
½ beaten egg

FOR THE LEMON FILLING
⅓ cup plus 1 tbsp (80 g) superfine
    sugar
2 large eggs plus 3 egg yolks (keep
    the egg whites!)
juice and grated zest of 2 lemons
5 tbsp (80 g) unsalted butter, at
    room temperature, cut into
    pieces

OR

FOR THE PINK GRAPEFRUIT FILLING
3 tbsp (40 g) sugar
2 large eggs plus 3 egg yolks (keep
    the egg whites!)
juice and grated zest of 1 pink
    grapefruit
juice and grated zest of ½ lemon
5 tbsp (80 g) unsalted butter, at
    room temperature, cut into
    pieces

FOR THE MERINGUE
3 large egg whites
pinch of salt
¾ cup (150 g) superfine sugar

Make the dough. This is ideally done in a food processor, but you can do it in a bowl as long as your hands are cold: Combine the flour, salt, and sugar. Add the butter and pulse until the dough looks like coarse crumbs. Add the egg and a few drops of ice-cold water. Pulse until the dough just comes together. Shape the dough into a flat slab, wrap it in plastic wrap, and chill in the fridge for 1 hour.

Make the lemon or grapefruit filling: In a small saucepan over low heat, combine the sugar, whole eggs and yolks, and juice and zest. Cook, stirring constantly, until it thickens and comes to a boil. As soon as it boils, add all the butter and whisk vigorously until you have a nice thick sauce. Remove from the heat and let cool.

Grease a shallow 9-inch (24-cm) tart pan with butter and line the bottom with parchment paper. Butter the paper. On a floured counter, roll out the dough into a nice thin slab large enough to cover the bottom and sides of the pan.

Press the dough into the pan and trim the edges with a sharp knife. Prick holes in the dough with a fork and place the pan in the freezer for at least 30 minutes.

Preheat the oven to 350°F (170°C).

Bake the tart shell in the bottom of the oven for 25 to 30 minutes, until golden brown.

Let cool for at least 15 minutes, then spread the lemon or grape-fruit filling in the tart.

Make the meringue: Preheat the broiler.

In a large, ultra-clean bowl, beat the egg whites with the salt. Add the sugar a little at a time, beating constantly and waiting until each batch of sugar is dissolved before adding the next. Beat until the whites are glossy and smooth and stand in firm peaks. Spoon the whites into a pastry bag, ideally one with a decorating tip. Pipe pretty Parisian dollops over the entire surface of the tart.

(If you don't have a pastry bag, you can use a spatula to dollop the meringue on the tart and create high peaks. That's pretty too.)

Place the tart under the broiler for 3 to 4 minutes, until the peaks turn brown.

Serve immediately. Isn't it super?

summer pudding

In Home Made Winter *I gave you the winter version of this pudding, but this is the original. You can use any combination of about 3½ pints (1.25 kg) mixed berries, but this is my favorite combination.*

1 pint (300 g) fresh strawberries, hulled and halved (big ones quartered)
⅔ pint (250 g) fresh blackberries
⅓ pint (100 g) fresh red currants
1½ pints (500 g) fresh raspberries
¾ cup plus 2 tbsp (175 g) superfine sugar
3 tbsp freshly squeezed lemon juice
7 square slices stale white bread
crème fraîche or sour cream for serving

Keeping the strawberries separate, wash the berries and carefully pat them dry with a paper towel.

In a large saucepan over medium heat, combine the sugar and lemon juice and bring to a gentle boil. Cook until the sugar is dissolved, stirring occasionally.

Add all the fruit except the strawberries and boil for 3 minutes tops, stirring, until the berries are soft and release their juices.

Place a sieve over a bowl and pour in the fruit. Reserve the fruit and the juices.

Line a 2-cup (500-ml) pudding mold with plastic wrap, letting the plastic overhang the sides. Remove the crust from 5 of the bread slices. Halve them lengthwise. Cut out a circle from the sixth slice to match the size of the bottom of the pudding mold.

Dip each cut slice of bread for 1 second in the fruit juice you collected in the bowl and use the slices to line the mold, the rectangular slices for the sides, the circle for the bottom.

Stir the strawberries into the rest of the fruit and fill the mold with the fruit.

Cut out a circle from the last slice of bread to match the size of the open top of the mold, dip it into the fruit juice, and use it to cover the pudding. Pull the plastic wrap over the top of the pudding and place something heavy directly onto the pudding. (I have a saucer that fits perfectly and I put a can of beans on top of that.)

Place in the fridge overnight, or for at least 6 or 7 hours.

Strain the remaining fruit syrup and save it in a little pitcher in the refrigerator.

Before serving, open up the plastic and place a large plate on top of the mold. Holding the plate onto the mold, invert the pudding onto the plate. Lift off the mold and remove the plastic wrap.

Serve summer pudding in wedges, with crème fraîche or sour cream and some of the fruit syrup.

molten chocolate cakes "en cocotte" with raspberries

It's heavenly, this dessert! Chocolate with raspberries is a popular combination—and with good reason. Or you could use passion fruit—a bit old-fashioned, maybe, but what's wrong with that?

FOR THE RASPBERRY SAUCE

½ cup (125 g) frozen raspberries
2 tbsp (25 g) sugar
juice of ½ lemon
2 tbsp Framboise (raspberry liqueur),
    if you wish

FOR THE MOLTEN CAKE

3 oz (80 g) dark chocolate
¾ cup (170 g) unsalted butter, plus
    more for the ramekins
1 tbsp milk
seeds from 1 vanilla bean
¼ cup (30 g) all-purpose flour
¼ cup (50 g) packed brown sugar
3 tbsp (40 g) almond flour
2 large eggs, separated

Make the raspberry sauce: Combine all the ingredients in a small saucepan and bring to a boil. Lower the heat and simmer for about 3 minutes, until the raspberries are broken down. Puree the raspberries briefly with an immersion blender and let the sauce cool completely. Place in the fridge until ready to use.

Make the molten cakes: Preheat the oven to 350°F (170°C). Generously butter 4 single-serving ramekins or ovenproof dishes. In the top of a double boiler (or in a bowl set on top of a saucepan of simmering water; make sure the water doesn't touch the bowl), melt the chocolate. Stir in the milk and the vanilla bean seeds.

Remove from the heat and stir in the flour, brown sugar, and almond flour. Beat the egg yolks until foamy and fold these in too.

In a separate, squeaky-clean bowl, beat the egg whites until firm peaks form, then gently fold them into the chocolate mixture.

Pour the batter into the prepared ramekins. Bake for 20 minutes, or until the edges are firm and the center is still soft.

Poke a hole in the center of each molten cake, pour in the cold raspberry sauce, and serve immediately!

pomegranate & pear–lime rockets

FOR AT LEAST 8 ICE ROCKETS

FOR THE PEAR–LIME ICE

2 ripe pears (12 oz / 350 g), peeled
    and cored
juice and grated zest of 1 lime
3 tbsp sugar

FOR THE POMEGRANATE ICE

¾ cup plus 1 tbsp (200 ml)
    pomegranate juice
1 orange, peeled and quartered
⅓ cup plus 1 tbsp (75 g) packed light
    brown sugar

Make the pear-lime ice: Combine all the ingredients in a blender and puree until smooth. Pour the puree into a measuring cup with a spout and let stand for 15 minutes to allow the sugar to dissolve.

Make the pomegranate ice: In a clean blender, combine all the ingredients and puree until smooth. Let stand for 15 minutes as well so the sugar can dissolve.

Pour about half of the pear mixture into ice-pop molds. Place in the freezer for 1 hour. Then distribute all of the pomegranate mixture in a layer on top of the frozen pear mixture, and freeze for another hour.

Insert the sticks and top off with the rest of the pear mixture. Freeze for 6 to 8 hours.

irish–coffee ice cream

6 large egg yolks
1 cup (200 g) packed light brown
   sugar
2 cups (500 ml) milk
¾ cup (175 ml) strong brewed
   coffee
3½ tbsp (50 ml) Irish whiskey

In a large bowl, combine the egg yolks and brown sugar and beat with an electric mixer until nicely foamy; whip for a long time so you get a good thick, foamy mixture. In a medium saucepan over low heat, warm the milk to lukewarm, pour in the coffee, then pour this mixture into the foamy egg yolks, stirring constantly. Pour all of this back into the saucepan and cook over medium heat, stirring constantly, until you have a nice thick sauce the consistency of custard. Remove from the heat and let cool to lukewarm. Stir in the whiskey and let cool completely. To keep a skin from forming, you can place a piece of plastic wrap or parchment paper directly on the surface of the custard.

Once the custard is cool, place it in a freezer-safe container, covered, in the freezer. Whisk it every hour until you have ice cream.

If you're the lucky owner of a ice-cream maker, you can turn the custard into ice cream in half an hour. Just follow the manufacturer's directions.

Serve with melted chocolate and slivers of honeycomb candy, or with fresh strawberries and whipped cream.

tips:

* Once the mixture has cooled off, spoon in some coarsely grated chocolate.

* Replace the whiskey with a few spoonfuls of liqueur. The recipe for coffee liqueur is in *Home Made*, in case you have that book as well, or just come up with something yourself. Be sparing with the alcohol, as too much alcohol or sugar will prevent ice cream from freezing. If you're so inclined, you can also just add a splash of some liqueur or other on top of the ice cream when you serve it.

honeycomb candy

5 tbsp sugar
2 tbsp golden syrup or honey
1 tbsp cold water
1 tbsp baking soda
a piece of dark chocolate, if you wish

Oil a small baking dish with vegetable oil. In a small saucepan over medium heat, combine the sugar and syrup and stir until the sugar melts. Lower the heat and cook without stirring until you have a tea-colored syrup. About 15 minutes.

Remove from the heat, add 1 tbsp cold water and the baking soda at once, and beat vigorously. The caramel will foam ferociously—that's okay. Beware, it's scorching hot—don't try to taste it.

Pour it over a greased baking sheet. Let cool completely, then break the candy into pieces. Crumble over ice cream or melt some chocolate, dip the honeycomb in the chocolate, and let it cool on parchment paper.

Eat honeycomb rather soon after it's cooled, at least within a day. Due to the humidity in the air, it will become sticky and slowly turn soft. Keep it in an airtight container.

white wine sorbet ice

1¼ cups (250 g) superfine sugar
1 cup (250 ml) sweet white wine,
    such as dessert Muscat
juice of 1 orange
juice of 2 lemons

In a medium saucepan over medium heat, bring the sugar, wine, and 1½ cups (350 ml) water to a boil slowly, stirring until the sugar is dissolved.

Let the mixture boil down until it's syrupy, about 10 minutes. Transfer to a freezer-safe container and let cool completely. Stir in the orange and lemon juice.

Cover the container and place it in the freezer. With a fork, beat the mixture every hour for 4 hours into a nice sorbet ice. (Or you can freeze it in an ice-cream maker according to the manufacturer's directions.)

Eat it on its own, or with fresh fruit, or maybe with the apricots in muscat syrup on page 238.

watermelon granita

1¾ lb (750 g) peeled and seeded
    watermelon, diced
1-inch (2-cm) piece of fresh ginger,
    peeled and sliced
¾ cup (150 g) sugar
leaves from 3 sprigs of mint
juice and grated zest of 1 lime

Combine all the ingredients in a blender and puree until smooth. Pour into a freezer-safe container. Cover the container and place it in the freezer for about 4 hours, beating it with a fork every hour, until it forms nice coarse ice crystals.

Scrape the granita with a fork before serving and spoon it into pretty, chilled coupes. Serve immediately; it melts quickly.

Cavaillon

"mousse au chocolat" with cherry–pink peppercorn sauce & lemon thins

No cookbook can come off the press without a recipe for chocolate mousse! Chocolate and fruit go well together because the fresh taste of the fruit balances so nicely with creamy chocolate. Chocolate and raspberries, for example, are a classic combination (see page 226), but cherries also work well, especially with pink peppercorns—you should really try it.

FOR THE CHOCOLATE MOUSSE
4 large eggs, separated
3 tbsp brown sugar
7 oz (200 g) good-quality dark
    chocolate, chopped
½ cup plus 2 tbsp (150 ml) heavy
    cream

FOR THE CHERRY SAUCE
1 cup (150 g) fresh cherries, pitted
1 tbsp pink peppercorns
3 tbsp sugar
½ tbsp cornstarch
1 generous tbsp freshly squeezed
    lemon juice

Make the chocolate mousse: In a large bowl, beat the egg whites until they're almost stiff. Add the brown sugar a little at a time and beat until the sugar is dissolved and the egg whites hold stiff peaks.

Melt the chocolate in the top of a double boiler (or in a bowl set on top of a saucepan of simmering water; make sure the water doesn't touch the bowl). In a small bowl, whisk the egg yolks with about 3 tbsp (50 ml) of the cream. Whisk this into the melted chocolate until thoroughly combined.

In a third bowl, whip the remaining cream until soft peaks form.

Gently fold first the chocolate mixture and then the egg whites into the whipped cream. Pour the mousse into a nice serving bowl, a soup terrine, or individual glasses, cover with plastic wrap, and put in the fridge for at least 3 hours to firm up.

Make the cherry sauce: In a small saucepan over medium heat, combine the cherries, peppercorns, sugar, and ½ cup (120 ml) water. In a small bowl, stir the cornstarch into the lemon juice until the cornstarch is dissolved and stir it into the sauce in the pan. Cook just until the sauce thickens, then remove from the heat and let cool completely.

Serve the cold cherry sauce with the chocolate mousse and lemon thins.

lemon thins

2 large eggs
½ cup plus 2 tbsp (125 g) sugar
1 tsp vanilla extract, or 2 tsp vanilla
    sugar
grated zest of 1 lemon
6 tbsp (85 g) unsalted butter
¾ cup (85 g) all-purpose flour
pinch of salt

Preheat the oven to 400°F (200°C). Line a baking sheet with parchment paper.

In a medium bowl, beat the eggs, sugar, and vanilla with an electric mixer for 5 minutes, until nice and foamy. Beat in the lemon zest.

In another bowl, beat the butter until light and airy. Alternately stir the butter and the flour in small batches into the egg mixture. Stir in a tiny pinch of salt.

Using two teaspoons, arrange small mounds of batter on the prepared baking sheet at least 2 inches (5 cm) apart (they'll spread in the oven).

Bake for about 5 minutes, or until the edges begin to brown.

Let the cookies cool on the pans for a few minutes, then use a thin spatula to transfer them to a rack to cool completely.

APRICOTS IN MUSCAT SYRUP WITH THYME + BAY LEAF

WITH A SHARP KNIFE, SCORE A CROSS IN THE SKINS OF 2 LB (1 KG) APRICOTS.

BRING A LARGE SAUCEPAN OF WATER TO A BOIL & ADD THE APRICOTS. COOK FOR 2-3 MINS. GENTLY SPOON THEM OUT.

RINSE THEM IMMEDIATELY UNDER COLD RUNNING WATER AND RUB OFF THE SKINS. ——→ BE CAREFUL.

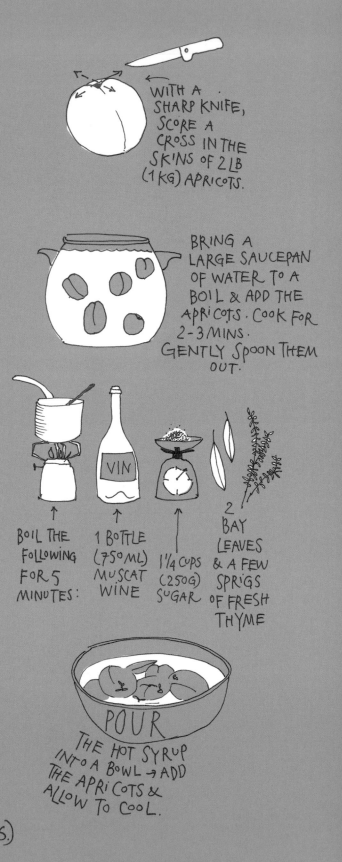

BOIL THE FOLLOWING FOR 5 MINUTES:

1 BOTTLE (750 ML) MUSCAT WINE

1 1/4 CUPS (250 G) SUGAR

2 BAY LEAVES & A FEW SPRIGS OF FRESH THYME

THE APRICOTS WILL KEEP FOR A FEW DAYS IN THE FRIDGE IF COVERED IN SYRUP → SO MAKE A LOT! THEY ARE NICE SERVED ON THEIR OWN, OR WITH ICE CREAM (OR THE WHITE WINE SORBET ON PAGE 233) OR WITH QUARK (PAGE 16).

(YOU CAN ALSO DO THIS WITH PLUMS, PEACHES OR NECTARINES.)

POUR THE HOT SYRUP INTO A BOWL → ADD THE APRICOTS & ALLOW TO COOL.

goat's milk yogurt parfait with cranberry crunch

FOR THE CRUNCH
½ cup (100 g) packed brown sugar
⅓ cup (50 g) all-purpose flour
7 tbsp (100 g) unsalted butter
⅔ cup (100 g) dried cranberries
  (keep a few aside for garnish)
½ cup (50 g) rolled oats

FOR THE PARFAIT
¾ cup (150 g) sugar
2 large egg yolks
1 vanilla bean, seeds scraped
¾ cup plus 1 tbsp (200 ml) milk
¾ cup plus 1 tbsp (200 ml) heavy
  cream
¾ cup plus 1 tbsp (200 ml) plain
  goat's milk yogurt

Make the crunch: Preheat the oven to 350°F (180°C). Line a baking sheet with parchment paper. Combine all the ingredients in a food processor and pulse until crumbly. Spread the mixture out over the baking sheet into a large, flat cookie.

Bake for about 20 minutes, until it's crunchy and golden brown. Let cool completely.

Make the parfait: Line a 5-by-9-inch (1-l) loaf pan with plastic wrap and let the edges overhang.

In a large bowl, beat the sugar with the egg yolks until you have very stiff white foam.

In a small saucepan over medium heat, combine the milk and the vanilla bean pod and seeds and bring to a simmer. Reduce the heat to low and cook for 10 minutes. Remove the vanilla bean and gradually stir the milk into the egg yolk mixture, stirring constantly, then pour the mixture back into the saucepan. Cook over low heat, stirring constantly, until the custard is as thick as thin yogurt. Remove from the heat.

Whip the cream to soft peaks.

Gently fold the whipped cream and yogurt into the custard and pour one third of it into the prepared loaf pan. Pulse the crunch briefly in a food processor to make crumbs and sprinkle half of it over the custard mixture, pour the rest of the parfait mixture on top, and reserve the remaining crunch for garnish. Cover the parfait with the plastic wrap overhanging the sides. Place in the freezer overnight.

Just before serving, lift the parfait gently out of the pan. Slice, place on chilled plates, and divide the rest of the cranberry crunch crumbles and reserved cranberries among the plates.

prosecco and elderflower jelly with melon

I grew up with jelly and cream. Again and again, at every children's birthday party in Ireland. Or worse: jelly and ice cream! Brrr. As a child I strongly disliked the combination of the light jelly and the creamy whipped cream or ice cream, and I still don't fancy it.

I do like jelly by itself, though. Most Dutch people never eat it, but it's so beautiful and light for dessert, so fresh and fruity after a heavy meal or at a barbecue—I'm going to convince you to try it.

FOR A 4-CUP (1-L) MOLD

4 sheets unflavored gelatin
2 tbsp elderflower syrup
1 cup (200 g) sugar
3 cups (700 ml) prosecco (Italian
    sparkling wine)
1 cantaloupe or honeydew melon
edible (white) pansies (available at
    specialty grocers), or unsprayed
    rose petals, daisies, or edible
    white carnations (that's what I
    used for this picture)

Put the gelatin sheets in a small saucepan and cover with cold water. Let stand for 5 minutes to soften. Remove the sheets from the pan and squeeze out excess water. Set aside.

In a separate saucepan over medium-high heat, combine the elderflower syrup with 1¼ cups (300 ml) water and the sugar and boil it down for about 10 minutes. Remove from the heat. Stir the softened gelatin sheets into the syrup, let it cool slightly, then add the prosecco and stir well. Set aside.

Scoop small balls from the melon. Put them in a 4-cup (1-l) mold or bowl. Add the flowers.

Pour in the gelatin liquid, cover the bowl with plastic wrap, and place in the fridge for at least 4 hours to firm up.

To get the jelly out of its mold, fill a larger bowl with hot water. Gently lower the mold into the water to warm it. Not too long, or the jelly will melt, and make sure the water doesn't overflow into the mold, as that will melt the jelly as well. When you see the sides come loose, it's time. Place a plate upside down on the mold, invert it, and the jelly should slowly and carefully slide out of its bowl.

If that doesn't work, warm the mold a little longer and try again. Serve immediately. Without cream.

nougat

It's fun to make nougat. Depending on the humidity in the air, it will need to dry for a shorter or longer period than I have indicated, so keep that in mind. You can also use other nuts like pistachios or hazelnuts, even pine nuts, or stir in some cocoa powder—you'll be surprised what you'll come up with yourself.

1. boil 1¾ cups plus 2 tbsp (375 g) sugar, 1 cup (250 ml) golden syrup or honey, ½ cup (125 ml) water, and a pinch of salt until the sugar is dissolved. Boil without stirring for about 15 minutes, until the syrup reaches 240°F (116°C) (the soft ball stage, it's called). **2. use** an electric mixer to beat an egg white until firm peaks form, then, beating constantly, pour in the hot syrup in a steady stream; the mixture will thicken and expand. Stir in ⅔ cup (50 g) candied cherries (chopped, if you wish), 2 cups (250 g) toasted almonds, and 1 tsp vanilla extract. **3. pour** the nougat into a greased rimmed baking sheet. Let cool briefly, then knead the nougat and shape it into a nice thick rectangle. **4. let** it dry for at least 24 hours, then cut it into slices. Store in an airtight container between layers of parchment paper.

financiers

Financiers aren't ordinary cakes. The browned butter and the egg white turn them into indescribably delicate, airy almond treats. You can buy them on every Paris street corner, but I don't see them much in the Netherlands. They're the easiest cakes in the world to make yourself. Pretty crazy, huh?

FOR ABOUT 16, DEPENDING ON
THE SIZE OF YOUR MOLD

½ cup plus 2 tbsp (150 g) unsalted
    butter
⅓ cup plus 1 tbsp (50 g) all-purpose
    flour
1½ cups (150 g) confectioners' sugar
½ cup (60 g) almond flour or finely
    ground almonds
pinch of salt
3 egg whites

Preheat the oven to 400°F (200°C). Thoroughly grease your financier pans. Heat the butter in a small saucepan over medium-low heat until the solids sink to the bottom of the pan in small crumbs and the fat becomes nicely dark and hazelnut colored and clear. This takes about 15 minutes, maybe a bit longer. Remove from the heat. (This is *beurre noisette*—browned butter.)

In a bowl, combine the flour, confectioners' sugar, almond flour, and salt. Pour in the melted butter (leaving the solids in the pan, though it's fine if a few come along). Add the egg whites and mix with a spatula to make a smooth batter.

Pour the batter into the prepared pans and bake for about 12 minutes (depending on the size of your pans—check them frequently!), until golden brown.

You can eat them after they've cooled for 5 minutes.

Have you ever eaten something so simple and so delicious?

Paris, France

recipe index

Marie

general index

Honeycomb candy, page 230

MERCI,
THANK YOU &
DANK JE WEL

O.O.F, LOVEDELUXE

*JORIS! * SOPHIE, ALEX, JESSICA
AND ALL THE OTHER AAN DE AMSTELS

MARIA, SOURCE OF HEAPS OF RECIPES AND STORIES
WIM, SOURCE OF REAL VEGETABLES AND STORIES

LA FAMILLE COLOMBET: CHARLES, GEORGES, NORBERT,
VALERIE, CRIS ET LES AUTRES > BISOUS

S.O.S. & LISTENING EAR: SOPHIE, GOOSJE AND HORAS AND
MY TONS OF SUPER-GREAT FRIENDS

MARTIN, VERA, INGE, BARTINA, ANNE MICHIEL, HENNIE AND ALL AT
FONTAINE * LESLIE, NATALIE, MARISA, AND EVERYONE AT ABRAMS

AND THE MOTHERS . . . AS YOU NEED TO LEARN HOW TO COOK AT SOME POINT. XXX

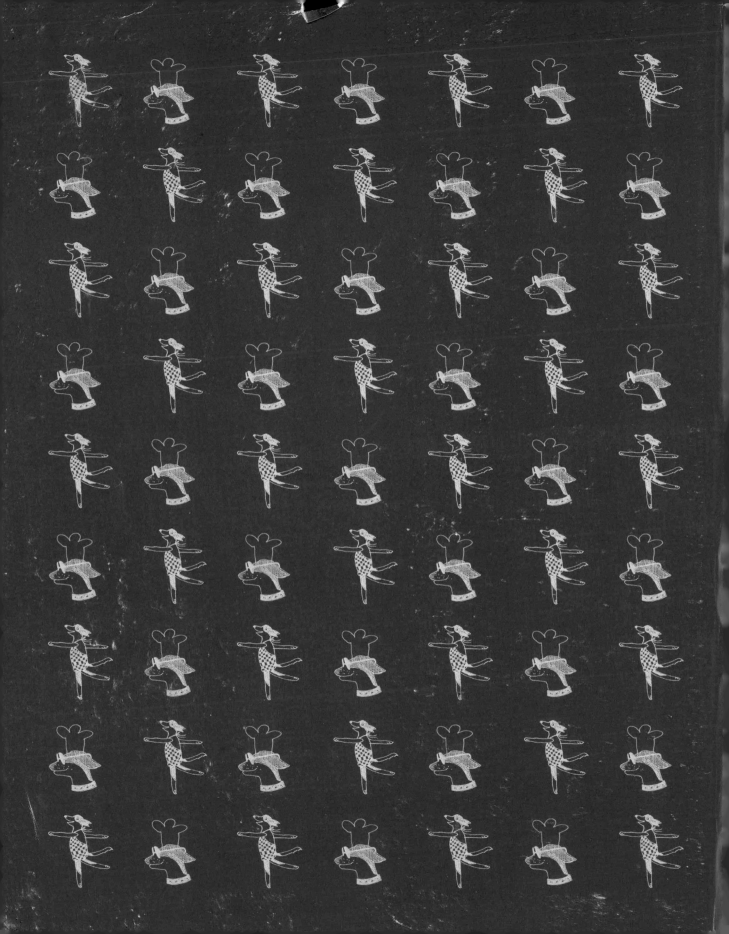